Equitable By Design

A GUIDE TO UTILIZING THE ABUNDANCE OF RESOURCES WITHIN BLACK FAMILIES AND COMMUNITIES TO SUPPORT STUDENTS

Yvette C. Latunde

Copyright © 2021 Kaleidoscope Vibrations, LLC

All rights reserved. No part of this publication may be reproduced or transmitted in any form or by any means, electronic or mechanical, including photocopy, recording, or any information storage and retrieval system, without permission in writing from the publisher.

Requests for permission to make copies of any part of this book should be emailed to:

publishing.kvibrations@gmail.com

Printed in the United States of America.

ISBN 978-1-949949-04-9

Cover design & book design by Caroline Rinaldy.

Cover images courtesy of Katerina Holmes and Monstera. Interior photos courtesy of Askar Abayev, Lukas Hartman, Aissa Bouabellou, Pedro, Charlotte May, R.F. Studio, Keira Burton, and Christina Morillo.

First printing, 2021

www.kvibrations.com

Praise for *Equitable By Design*

Instructive, empowering, and overwhelmingly positive. This wonderful resource should be used in schools and districts, across the nation, that are concerned with partnering with Black families and communities, in order to increase student achievement. Equitable by Design is user-friendly, extremely practical, and connects councils with valuable information.

— Amber Lynwood, Ed.D.,
Assistant Professor, Division of Teacher
Education, Azusa Pacific University

A brilliant piece of work with actionable insights to achieve Black student success informed by real insight of Black families.

The well organized framework exposing traditional parent involvement with the reality of how black families engage for their students' success is a must read for school administrators and educational leaders alike. A refreshing and real reflection of what Black families value in terms of schools and advocating for equitable education.

— Melessa Hamilton,
Middle School Teacher,
African American Parent Council Member

This interactive, user-friendly guidebook is an essential tool for all school systems. This guidebook is grounded in sound theoretical frameworks and guiding principles. Educators will be empowered and equipped to take an asset-based approach to strengthening relationships with Black families and authentically engaging them as true partners in their children's education.

— Cynthia Glover-Woods,
Member, California State Board of Education

Schools and organizations serving Black children and families need this guidebook. Dr. Latunde provides a practical guide for educators, community members, and parents to evaluate their policies and practices and co-create new processes with families in order to ensure Black students' success. With this guidebook, Dr. Latunde has provided tools and strategies educators can employ to see to it every student succeeds.

— Dr. Rema Vassar,
Michigan State Trustee, Associate Professor of Leadership and Counseling,
Eastern Michigan University

This book is relatable, thought-provoking, and very helpful to stakeholders such as educators, administrators, and university professors. Welcoming advice is provided to help Black families and students feel safe in a classroom setting. The plethora of guiding questions, action steps, ways to promote hospitality, joy, and relationship building is written with intentionality and purpose.

— Dr. Ie May Freeman, Assistant Professor of School of Education, Azusa Pacific University

This is a must-read resource book for anyone interested in helping Black and African American children reach their full academic potential.

— Dr. Greg Richardson, Director, Watson and Associates Literacy Center, California State University

A well designed and organized guide for practitioners who wish to engage Black students and families. The practical tools provided throughout this guide will be beneficial to educators who aim to go beyond involving their Black families to engaging Black families.

— Dr. Talisa Sullivan, CEO and Founder, Transformational Leadership Consulting

Dedication

First, I would like to dedicate this book to my parents, Omie M. Cormier and Lawrence J. Cormier. Without your examples of love, family, and community, there would be no book.

I would also like to dedicate this book to all of the parents, family, and community members who work effortlessly to engineer experiences, gather resources, and make the most of what they have to not only support their children, but the children of the larger community.

Lastly, this book is dedicated to all of those working in schools that take the time to make hospitality a priority. Thank you for the kind words, the warm tones, the eye contact, and the authentic invitations to be a part of schools.

Table of Contents

Preface xi
Introduction xiii
1 - Family Engagement 1
2 - Guiding Principles 19
3 - Guiding Frameworks 29
4 - What's the Big Idea?! 45
5 - Coming to an Agreement 51
6 - District-Level Advisory Councils 57
7 - Advisement 63
8 - Capacity Building 69
9 - Yearly Practice Ideas 79
10 - Monthly Experiences 91
11 - Messaging 97
12 - Recognizing and Using Strengths 103
13 - Interactive and Interdependent Work 107
Conclusion 133
Appendices 135
Acknowledgements 143
About the Author 149
References 151
Index 155

Preface

Equitable by Design examines the possibilities for building more equitable, culturally informed, and evidence-based partnerships among Black families, communities, and schools. The processes and practices recommended in this guide are grounded in theory. That theory is translated into evidence-based practices associated with improved student outcomes for Black students. This guide also recognizes and respects "other ways of knowing," or people's lived experiences, understanding that science is still catching up on its knowledge of what works for historically marginalized groups. This book invites participation in creating welcoming environments for Black families and their children. It provides processes that begin with the abundance within families and communities in mind, transfers power, builds capacity, and fosters collective responsibility and collective decision-making. These processes offer the possibilities for increasing the safety and belonging of Black families and students, improving student learning and well-being, transforming systems within schools, and developing strategic partnerships that build upon the knowledge, expertise, and experiences of Black people.

Book Features:

- Broadens the concept of leadership in schools to include Black families, students, and community members
- Explores processes for creating safe and hospitable environments for Black families to engage with schools
- Shares a range of concepts, strategies, and practices for utilizing partnerships with families, communities, and schools to support student success and well-being
- Translates theory into evidence-based practices that support diverse families and community engagement
- Provides opportunities for individual and team reflection
- Focuses on goal setting and action steps
- Explores culturally modified evidence-based practices to effectively engage families and support students
- Provides step-by-step guidance for Black Family Advisory Councils with Dr. Yvette C. Latunde

Introduction

"When we only name the problem, when we state complaint without a constructive focus or resolution, we take hope away. In this way critique can become merely an expression of profound cynicism, which then works to sustain dominator culture"

(bell hooks, *Teaching Community: A Pedagogy of Hope*)

Welcome, courageous leaders.

This guidebook was created just for you, whether you are an educator, advocate, parent or guardian, or simply a conscientious citizen. This book introduces you to—or reminds you of—the abundance within Black families, neighborhoods, and communities that can be used to strengthen Black children and youth. It guides you in using that abundance to support the academic success and well-being of Black students in schools.

If you are reading this book because you want to know how to start a Black Family Advisory Council or how to enhance your existing parent advisory, you are in the right place. If you are reading it because you want to know what you can do to support Black students in schools, you are in the right place. This work has been effective in places where there are a large number of Black students, as well as in places where Black students constitute a very small percentage of the student population. The exciting news is that what works well with Black students works well for most students. The converse has not been found to be true. This guidebook was created to give you action steps for using the individual and collective strengths of Black families and communities to improve schools for Black students.

If you would like more theory on the topic and on how to conduct research on parental engagement, consider my book, *Research in Parental Involvement: Methods and Strategies for Psychology* (published by Palgrave). But if you are ready to *do something* that will better the lives of Black students, read on.

This guidebook is a wealth of information. It contains much of what I have learned as I have worked with hundreds of families, dozens of communities, over 50 school districts, and scores of faith-based and community organizations. It condenses more than 12 years of experience working with Black Family Councils into a simple format for you to use. It is packed with information about Black families: on the concepts and practices they value; the ways they support their children's learning; what makes them feel safe and welcomed; the strength of their connections; what they consider engagement with schools to be. It contains information about schools and the people who run them—how they think and how they work. It is filled with practical information regarding hospitality, physical space, structures and policies, and recognizing and building on the myriad strengths of the Black community.

This guidebook is a roadmap for change. It does more than present information; it asks questions and gives space for reflection so that you can consider how the information relates to your situation and your concerns. It guides you through a process of determining the specific actions you will take to support Black children and families.

This guidebook has multiple uses for multiple people. If you are part of a Black Family Council, you can use it to strengthen your work. If you are a parent, grandparent, or guardian, you can use it to make your involvement in your child's education more effective. If you are a community member, you can follow the roadmap to create the conditions that enable your community and its children to thrive. There is something in this book for everyone. Take what *you* need and leave the rest for others. But do take. And use. Use what you read and write in these pages to make your schools and community better places for everyone.

For more advanced information or deeper learning on the topic, sign up for one of my courses or certification programs.[1]

What Brings Me to This Work?

My parents met on a college campus in the San Francisco Bay area of California in the 1960s. My mother, a native of Nacogdoches, Texas, was a top student

---

[1] Stay connected through www.bridgesleadership.com

in both high school and university. She is a musician, writer, dancer, entrepreneur and teacher. My father is from San Diego, California, by way of Houston, Texas. He is an American Air Force veteran, a martial arts expert, and a licensed mental health services professional who owned a private mental health services practice after retiring from a county department of mental health services.

After graduating from the university and beginning their respective careers—my mother as a university professor and my father as a therapist—my mother, with the support of my father and the participation of a few community stakeholders, co-founded a community school for Black, Hispanic, Chicano, and Latino/a/x students in 1978. The school operated for more than 37 years in Central California.

My mother's experiences attending integrated schools had been negative. Teachers doubted her intelligence, discouraged her from studying math, ignored her brilliance, and believed her "race" was a detriment to society. My mother did not want her children to be taught "by people who did not like them"; hence, she started the school.

My parents worked with a small group of community members including business owners, council members, city managers, parents, educators, and faith leaders to create a safe place where children of color could learn, play, and grow in the middle of a very disenfranchised and neglected community. Families of students and community members were always invited and welcomed to the 5.7-acre campus. Family and community were central to the health and uplift of the school. Key features of the school were: family and community volunteers; community service; a community garden;

Introduction

and an interactive process by which the community, students, and families shaped the school and the school shaped the community.

The campus was a safe place for everyone in the community. All sorts of community events took place there: church services, karate practices, music lessons, wedding receptions, and community meetings. Academically, over 90% of all students attending for more than three years tested above average on all standardized tests.

My siblings and I attended my mother's community school through eighth grade. During my high school and college years, my parents were very active in my growth and development both on and off campus. They spoke with teachers, advocated for me at the school site, provided tutoring, furnished me with resources on metacognition and mental health. They affirmed me, took me to college campuses for events of interest, paired me with mentors, modeled reading, instilled the importance of education, kept an active faith in God, enrolled me in a plethora of extracurricular activities, advised me on coursework, and provided financial support until I no longer needed it. All six of their children are college graduates with thriving careers and healthy relationships.

Because of this upbringing, I know Black families have strengths and are active in the growth and development of not only their own children, but other people's children as well. I have seen so many examples in my parents and other community members.

When I became a parent, these early experiences influenced how I conceptualized my role with schools and what I believed was possible. Circumstances were different, however. My children were not attending schools in the communities where I had grown up. Their teachers and school leaders were rarely part of the community in which they were teaching and leading. There were also clear dynamics at play involving power, race, class, age, gender, and socioeconomic status. In other words, there was great resistance to my engagement in my own children's schooling even though I am a credentialed teacher, school leader, and university professor.

These dynamics are rarely mentioned in the literature when we hear about a "lack of parent involvement" and "gaps in achievement." This work calls out those dynamics.

My parents before me experienced many of the same negative stereotypes and resistance I experienced. However, not engaging with schools was never an option for them, nor is it for me. So, we persist. Sad to say, in my work as a scholar who has studied family and community partnerships for 14 years, I see that the conditions of schools and anti-Blackness has not changed much from the days when my parents were students and the time when they co-founded a school.

I have helped to create, develop, and expand Black or African American parent councils in over thirty-three school districts. This guidebook presents some of the principles, frameworks, practices, and guidelines I have found to be useful.

What Brings You?

Once again, please note that this guidebook is not meant to be prescriptive, but rather supportive in helping you create, develop, or expand your work with Black students and families. It asks you to reflect on what is presented, considering how the material relates

Introduction

to the specifics of your context and situation. Use the **Reflections** spaces provided throughout the guidebook to record your thoughts, goals, and plans for your unique work.

This is a workbook. It invites you to take a number of concrete actions, writing goals, identifying needs and resources, naming names. Do the work, take the steps. The end—vibrant, effective, equitable partnerships that create equitable and humanizing schools in which Black children thrive—is worth it.

Reflections

What brings you to this work?

What's your story?

1

Family Engagement

"When people are included in the broader project, they become invested. This investment of time, knowledge, and resources serves to establish community understanding and kinship"

(Garcia et al., 2020, p. 92).

Family engagement with schools is a good concept. It is the idea that schools and families should work together to support the growth and development of children. However, many schools have situated Black parents as outsiders regarding their children's education. Black families have been pushed to the side in schools. This is demonstrated by many of the policies and practices that isolate parents, dismiss their concerns, and diminish their decision-making in the education of children and youth. A Black Family Advisory Council (BFAC) may help correct this if properly supported. Two White House initiatives highlight the importance of this work: (1) the January 2021 White House Executive Order on Advancing Racial Equity and Support for Underserved Communities and (2) the White House Initiative on

Educational Excellence for African Americans.[2] Two of the guiding principles in these orders are:

1. To highlight people, programs and practices facilitating the learning and development of African Americans students.

2. To serve as a liaison between and among communities supporting African American students of all ages.

Important Terms and Definitions

Language is important. It is important because this work with parents must be easily accessible. At the same time, those leading this work must become familiar with the language commonly used in schools. The BFAC needs to use plain language when working with families to ensure that the council does not reinforce classism. I invite leaders of this work to be mindful about terms such as parent, family, Black, African American, meeting, gathering, or social. Each term communicates a specific tone and intent.

Work with your families and schools to determine what language best fits your intentions and needs. The first area for clarification is how the council will define parental involvement and family engagement. It is perfectly acceptable to combine ideas and perspectives if they meet your needs.

Here are a few operational definitions for **family engagement**:

---

[2] To learn more about White House Initiative on Educational Excellence for African Americans, visit https://sites.ed.gov/whieeaa/

- Parents' belief about what they are supposed to do (Hoover-Dempsey & Sandler, 1995)
- Parents helping their children succeed (Hoover-Dempsey & Sandler, 1995)
- Shared decision-making (Pushor, 2017)
- Attending meetings, volunteering, subtle (Jeynes, 2003)
- Supplementing learning, racially socializing, sharing decision-making, encouraging, modeling (Latunde, 2017)
- Helping to co-design, implement, and reflect upon school interventions (Ishimaru, 2019)

See the National Education Associations brief on Every Student Succeeds Act and Parent Involvement[3] for a quick guide to district responsibilities; see the Individuals with Disabilities Education Act (IDEA[4]) for Parent Participation in Special Education Processes and Programs.

Anti-Blackness refers to attitudes and actions that position Black people and their cultural practices and knowledge as inferior, sub-standard, or needing to imitate others.

Black is used to denote people of African descent and the African diaspora.

The terms **conventional** and **traditional** are used to describe involvement or engagement initiatives and practices used by schools that place schools in a position of power over families and communities. Schools

---

[3] https://ra.nea.org/wp-content/uploads/2016/06/FCE-in-ESSA-in-Brief.pdf

[4] https://sites.ed.gov/idea/regs/b/d/300.322

determine the agenda and families are expected to be respondents or passive participants. For example, Parent Teacher Association membership, attendance at meetings, volunteering, and fundraising are touted as good enough parental/family engagement.

Engagement is preferred over the term involvement. Engagement implies a partnership with families. It also positions schools as active participants in the outreach to families, acknowledging schools should learn about families, create safe and welcoming spaces for them, and create structures and policies that support their meaningful participation.

Here the term **equity** is referencing racial equity. It is corrective and justice-focused. It recognizes historical injustices while also interrupting contemporary ones.

The term **family** is used to acknowledge that more than the biological parents may be responsible for the education of youth and engagement with schools. This term centers the practices, knowledge, and experiences of Black people who have extended families and adopt people into their "tribes" or families as they deem fit. Recognizing this reality is especially important because non-custodial relatives or friends of the family, grandparents, and non-custodial biological relatives may be responsible for the care of children. This understanding of the term also recognizes the situation of Black children and youth in foster homes or other arrangements.

There are other terms used frequently in schools. *The Glossary of Education Reform* lists some of them. It would not be a bad idea to make learning these terms a part of the internal work of the council.

Black Families and Schools

> It is inappropriate to categorize any group as deviant, and therefore out of mainstream. Either conformity or non conformity may be effective responses to the situation in which a group finds itself, and either may be harmful or helpful depending on the situations of group members
>
> (Willie et al., 2010, p. 17).

Much of the success of Black students can be attributed to family and community engagement, a fact that demonstrates what is needed and useful for Black children and youth. Equally important are the collective focus and specific actions that ensure the well-being of Black students in their homes and their respective communities (Evans, 2021; Hill, 2003). Models of school reform that have been effective center the roles of families and communities of color in the academic success and well-being of Black students. In these models, families are not used as points of blame or labor; rather, they are consultants, partners, and supporters. These models increase opportunities for relationship and capacity building and normalize mutual respect, shared decision-making, and shared accountability. Two such models that have been well researched, developed, and tested are the *Comer School Developmental Model and Levine's Accelerated School Model* (Latunde, 2017). Other counter narratives that recognize the successes of Black students include *Learning While Black; There is Nothing Wrong with Black Students; Just Schools;* and *Young, Gifted and Black.*

Black students belong to complex communities. Their communities are rich with people, resources, ideas, experiences, and knowledge central to supporting Black children and youth (Arrington & Stevenson, 2006). Black people value many forms of education, including formal schooling. African American families have historically valued education and have a high expectation for their children to attend college (Allen & White-Smith, 2018; Bridges et al., 2012; Edwards, 1993; Mungo, 2013). They see themselves as integral to their children's educational success and want to be actively engaged in all aspects of their children's education (Bridges et al., 2012).

Schools that do well with Black children recognize this and have developed strategic and authentic partnerships with communities of color. They partner with after-school programs, faith-based organizations, coaches, and mentors to serve Black students. They work in communities and with families to learn and practice principles that increase safety and trust.

These partnerships inevitably shift the power, practices, perceptions, and norms in schools to better reflect a democracy and to value and care for Black children and youth. They also raise the community's trust in schools and those working in them. Partnerships can begin by having Black community members as part of the school's professional learning community, involving community members and Black students in the improvement of curriculum, and finding ways to jointly reflect and assess the individual and collective cultural competence of those working in schools (Khalifa, 2018). Communities can also help schools authentically embed representation and interrupt the policing, criminalization, and segregation of Black students.

The Law: Involvement vs. Engagement

"The strategic challenge is whether we can value regular citizens, non-systems people, and believe that they are competent to create new policy"

(McKnight et al., 2012, p. 107).

Family involvement is the law; family engagement is not. Family engagement is, however, vital to student success. In involvement, families agree to participate in activities that are coordinated by the school. Engagement is shared decision-making and leadership; in engagement, families are considered in the construction of all aspects of schooling. It is the distinction between these two that makes this work complex and, at times, challenging. The Every Student Succeeds Act has a specific mandate stating that schools must involve families. However, involvement is broadly defined with a lot of room for interpretation. The law states only that parents, and this could be one or two parents out of five hundred, must be involved in advisory and decision-making. The law does not say that Black families must be involved in advisory and decision-making. In other words, schools and districts are able to meet the parental involvement requirement without family engagement—that is, without the input, advice, approval, or cooperation of Black families. The law does specify that schools are mandated to seek the involvement of persons with children with disabilities, families that are low-income, and/or families of language learners. The National Board of State Educators has written more about this in its policy briefs.

In the work of Black Family Advisory Councils (BFACs), Black children and youth are the primary focus. A BFAC as an advisory group to schools and districts is a force that must be reckoned with. It is incumbent on schools or districts to seek the cooperation, advice, input, and perhaps approval of BFACs in making decisions that impact Black children and youth since the council exists for the betterment of all children. Engagement is a matter of equity.

A Word of Caution

Family engagement in schools is not the same as parenting. Family engagement is directly linked to activities connected to schooling to support children in their education. Engaging with schools is one of many parental responsibilities. A BFAC should not be used by schools, districts, or the council itself to evaluate or assess individual or group parenting. Advisory councils are not parenting groups. They are not to be used to critique and evaluate Black parents. The purpose of this work is to support Black student success by being student-focused, community- and family-centered, reflective and responsive, and data driven. BFACs work with external groups and individuals to present a collective and united voice about what is happening, what is needed, and what is helpful in supporting Black students toward their academic success and well-being. The councils seek to interrupt systems that are used in schools to isolate, harm, and depress the outcomes of Black children and youth.

Supporting Engagement

Based on the text, what would you say are the differences between family engagement and involvement?

What has been your experience with involvement or engagement in schools (Pre-schools - 12th grade)?

What do you notice about the laws related to family involvement and engagement?

What are some of the ways you can advocate for other people's children?

Build Upon, Don't Recreate

"The shift we seek begins when we declare that the properties (kindness, generosity, cooperation, forgiveness, mystery, acceptance) and capabilities that make up a competent community exist in human nature"

(McKnight et al., 2012, p. 68).

I am very familiar with the literature on Black family engagement and involvement. Although the mechanisms used to engage with schools may differ based on education, age, geographic location, income, grade level, and type of school, the literature indicates that Black families are active in the education of children and youth. An effective BFAC will build upon the strengths of Black families. Black families are already involved and engaged in their children's education in many ways. Knowing this fact is important because it establishes a strengths-based mindset and rejects deficit views of Black families. The chart below compares traditional forms of parent involvement with the nuanced ways Black families are involved and engaged.

Mechanisms Used	Traditional/ Conventional	Nuanced/Non-Traditional
Encouragement	Volunteering in schools	Racial socialization
Modeling	Attending meetings	Values
Reinforcement	PTA	Communicating goals

Mechanisms Used	Traditional/ Conventional	Nuanced/Non-Traditional
Direct instruction	Back to School Night/Open House	Engineering, facilitating, and expanding opportunities to develop social skills
Networks	Responding to school request	Shared decision-making
Community supports	Homework support	Supplementing education
Influences	Shared reading	Demonstrating care and value
Child's response to involvement and engagement	Modeling reading	Focus on mastery
Invitations to engage		Promoting college attendance
Culture		Establishing structure and discipline
Time & energy		Problem-solving with teachers
Ideas about their roles in schools		Advocating for teaching-learning fit
Personal skills and knowledge		Promoting extracurricular activities
Perceptions of safety and belonging		Advocating for all students
Child's individual personality and strengths		Reinforcing the authority of teachers and importance of schools
		Leading in schools
		Mental health

Why?

> "Jeynes (2005) found that involvement that required large amounts of time and was more subtle had a greater impact on educational outcomes than the more traditional and demonstrative forms of involvement"
>
> (Latunde, 2017, p.10).

    Clarity about the purpose of family engagement is important. The purpose of Black family engagement is to help create more equitable schools and humanized conditions for Black students. The purpose is not to have 150 family members at a social event. Rather, 150 families might attend board meetings over the course of a year to bring issues to the attention of the board and to request evidence-based solutions. Black family councils serve two main purposes: (1) promoting community among students, families, and schools and (2) co-designing solutions that benefit Black students. Thus, there is a larger purpose for family engagement that requires actions beyond attending meetings and events. Attendance at activities itself does not represent the full continuum of parental involvement or engagement. Attendance in meetings and events is loosely connected to the academic achievement of Black students. Is it important? Yes. But when schools share the responsibility of supporting Black students in the classrooms and leaders create structures that interrupt structural racism, that is when all students succeed. Therefore, a robust advisory council seeks to engage only in those conversations, activities, and initiatives that serve to decrease student and family isolation and increase support and services for Black students inside and outside of the schools.

Questions to ponder and discuss:

1. Why do we want family engagement?
2. What are our motivations for this work?
3. Does our reason match the school's/district's reason? How do we know?
4. How are we defining engagement? Or do we want involvement?
5. How will our involvement or engagement make schools better for students?
6. How can we collaborate to ensure evidence-based teaching practices are used?
7. How can we promote leadership practices to reduce gaps in schools?
8. How can we reduce student and family isolation?
9. Who are the community partners who have some of the same concerns?
10. Are we willing to grow as leaders, or should we become members?

Family Engagement

Reflections

Why does the team believe this council is important?

What are the district's/school's motivations to start a council? How do you know?

How might the council advocate for the academic success and well-being of Black students?

Family Engagement

Action

Based on what you have learned in this guide about terms and definitions related to family engagement and involvement, develop three short and concise working definitions for family engagement. Use a combination of terms and definitions if appropriate. These can be voted upon later and used to communicate what the council would like to see in terms of how the school works with Black families to support students.

1.

2.

3.

Equitable By Design

2

Guiding Principles

"Knowledge is not what some know and others do not: It is not a commodity that can be possessed or controlled by educational institutions, but a living process to be absorbed and understood"

(Battiste, 2020, p. 15).

Black family engagement centers Black knowledge, experience, and practices. Black people are very diverse, but they share several values. Black people value morality, social connections, religion, politics, aesthetics, hard work, integrity, congruence, and fiscal responsibility. Each and every interaction with Black families should be mindful of these values. The next figure illustrates five characteristics of family engagement based on these values that resonate well with Black families. Research has shown these characteristics to be effective foundations for partnering in schools. The characteristics can serve as guiding principles for family engagement.

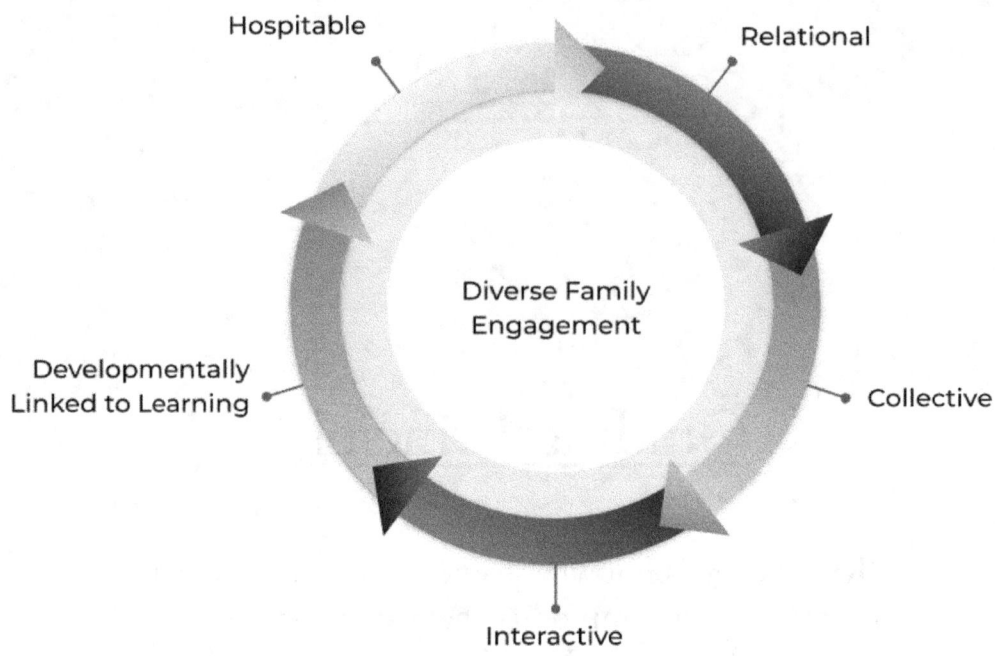

Hospitable

"Hospitality is the welcoming of strangers. There is always a welcome no matter how bonded the members of the community might be"

(McKnight et al., 2012, p. 78).

      Effective engagement of Black families is hospitable. That means the words and activities make Black families feel emotionally, physically, psychologically, and spiritually safe. What sorts of things do that? Black people value aesthetics. They are looking for representation in the people leading. It is important that messaging about what is normal, good, or pleasant is aligned

Guiding Principles

with their values and perspectives. Avoid perpetuating the imitation of Whiteness or of highly successful people from Asian descent who also prioritize Whiteness. Because we know Black people live under enormous amounts of stress and have been traumatized by generational racial and economic violence, we must embed healing-centered and culturally informed practices into this work. These practices may include yoga, prayer, meditation, music and movement, Qigong, grounding activities, story-telling and breath-work.

It is recommended that each and every gathering with Black families and students embed culturally informed healing-centered practices such as discharging activities and breath-work. Teacher education programs around the world are embedding mindfulness in their training of teachers and asking that teachers do the same with their students. I have noticed that it is better if Black students and families move or discharge energy with sensing activities or breath-work before they ground themselves. I recommend using mind-body practices such as Qigong, shaking, tapping, stomping, clapping, dancing, or walking. A discharging practice can be followed up with breath-work or a grounding activity. An example of a sensing activity is sitting comfortably and noticing things in your environment in detail and describing those things in writing.

To support the goals you have set for family and community engagement you can begin with an activity that will contribute to the engagement of Black families in your district or school. Below is a grounding activity for you to consider.

Grounding Activity (materials: families, paper, writing utensils, a timer etc.)

Ask families to look at their surroundings and identify and describe the following on paper:

- ▶ Five things they can see
- ▶ Four things they hear
- ▶ Three things they smell
- ▶ Two things they feel

A timer could be set for 30 to 60 seconds for writing each description. After the activity, ask the participants if they noticed anything or have them use one word to express how they experienced the activity.

For other grounding activity ideas, YouTube has many suggestions for short breathing exercises. The most common are inhaling through the nose (expanding the diaphragm) for 4 seconds and exhaling (emptying the diaphragm) through the mouth or nose for 6-8 seconds. Do this four times and then guide everyone to see if they notice anything or express how they feel.

Relational and Collective

"A competent community is focused on the gifts of its members, nurtures associational life, and offers hospitality"

(McKnight et al., 2012, p. 67).

Black people value relationships. Take time to intentionally promote relationship building, conflict resolutions and bonding. Relationships are based on trust, mutual respect, morals, ethics, and demonstration of an active concern with the poor treatment of

Black people. Trust is developed over time. People look for consistency, authenticity, and actions that support Black children and youth. Black people in the U.S. see themselves connected by common experiences. There are two key places in society where Black families develop, sustain, and maintain relationships outside of their own immediate families: in faith-based organizations/churches and in their respective communities. Their communities may include their immediate neighborhood; parks and recreation centers; Black family parenting groups; Black Greek organizations; honor, music, and art societies; Black MBA; National Association for the Advancement of Colored People; and other racial or gender-based networks.

People experience collective joys and sorrows when their communities are impacted. If there is something going on in the larger society related to Black people, all Black people are impacted by it. Do not ignore it; integrate it into the work. For example, the Black Lives Matter and Me Too movements cannot be separated from supporting Black students in schools.

Interactive and Developmentally Linked to Learning

This work is sure to attract a diverse group of people. Some will have a great deal of formal education; some will have experience in school settings; some will be passionate, willing, and ready to help in any way. The council seeks to create space where everyone feels valued, is safe, and has a sense of belonging. This means the council must create things for the people who show up and for those they want to show up. No one is interested in being a passive participant all the time. It is important that the council identify people's interests, strengths, mindsets, and skills and think about how they may be used to move Black students forward. This work is social, political, moral, ethical, and educational; therefore, any opportunity to build capacity in any of these areas—capacities that can be linked to student and family support—is beneficial to Black students.

I recommend using principles from Universal Design for Learning in this work. Focus on multiple means for presentation, engagement, and expression. Please see CAST.org for the most updated information on this framework. In a nutshell, the council wants to communicate in ways that resonate with the most people; this requires using multiple ways to communicate. Communication could be in the form of infographics, visuals, bullet points, or audio-visual presentations. Do not assume everyone learns by reading or hearing the material once. As a matter of fact, we remember 80% of what we teach to others and only 13% of what we hear. If you can create centralized sites with members-only access for all meetings, notes, flyers, and so forth, you will increase access and improve communication. With a central site, people can go back and review past information and materials.

Use multiple means to engage people. People love to learn with others and have fun. Even if the BFAC gathering is connected to a data-driven topic, consider ways to make the meeting engaging. Use simple graphics. Have someone there who can explain what the numbers mean. Create small groups to identify evidence-based solutions and groups that can work with families to implement the solutions. Think about using online materials; check the IRIS Center, a virtual warehouse with free educational and interactive resources, or the National Center for Urban School Transformation of San Diego State University for the most updated research on what works. Have small groups share their findings with the larger group for discussion and next steps. Using small groups may increase male representation in BFACs. I have learned that our work tends to be very conversational and less active. For balance we need more active engagement and fewer passive presentations.

Here is how you can use these guiding principles in your planning process.

Ask.....

1. Is this activity or event meaningful to families and Black students?
2. Does this promote interdependence and independence for families or students?
3. Is this activity or experience linked to learning?
4. Is there a balance of social and educational experiences and activities?
5. Are the offerings developmental (something for varying levels of education, experience, and capacity)?
6. Do the aesthetics reflect the community?
7. Are we mindful of the political and economic climate?
8. Is this a collective concern?
9. Is this interactive?
10. Does this increase the family's capacity to advocate?
11. Does this increase support and services for students?

Reflections

What makes you feel safe and welcome in a space?

How might people who are relational and collective behave differently from those who are more individualistic?

Guiding Principles

What are three ways to ensure our gatherings are relational, interactive, and linked to learning? Is there anyone who can help us with this?

What are three ways to ensure our gatherings are relational, interactive, and linked to learning?

3

Guiding Frameworks

"Hospitality generates from trust and produces trust. It is a source of generosity, vitality and learning"

(McKnight et al., 2012, p. 79).

There are two theories that guide this work: Hospitality and Capacity-Building.

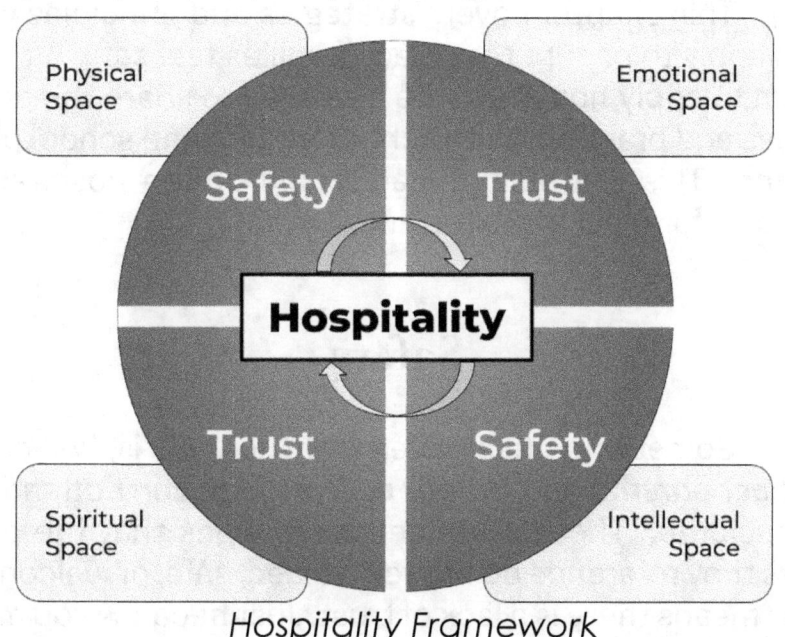

Hospitality Framework

To read more about the hospitality framework concept, see Latunde, 2017.

Hospitality is concerned with spiritual, physical, emotional, and intellectual safety. This framework is focused on creating safe spaces for Black and African American families in the council, schools, and district. This includes those from non-Black communities that are providing love and care for Black or African American students.

When people do not feel safe, they fight, freeze, or leave (flight). These are automatic responses to stress and threat. Black families live under considerable identity-based threats. The councils' first priority is to intentionally create places that are welcoming and safe for Black families. There are some general elements that make all people feel safe; however, working with Black families is nuanced. The typical approaches used with other parent groups have not been effective in creating safe spaces for Black families in schools and are strongly discouraged.

This chapter covers strategies and principles you can apply to ensure that Black families feel safe. As you learn to apply hospitality be prepared to share the principles and practices with school leaders and school personnel. This will build capacity and create hospitable schools for Black scholars and families.

Safety

Something I hear often from schools is, *"we cannot get parents out"* or *"our parents just won't attend or participate."* These statements are signs that the parents they reference do not feel valued, safe, or welcome. This means there is a lack of trust. Just because you may share a racial, cultural, and linguistic background with parents doesn't mean the parents will trust you or the council. Trust is built over time. I invite you to find two or three parents who are highly motivated and willing to take this journey with you. Start small.

This is what I have learned about families and safety: safety is both perception and reality. In other words, if people believe they are safe, their bodies respond by resting, self-regulating, digesting, and bonding. If they perceive danger, the nervous system responds as if they are stressed and under actual threat. Those responses are called fight, flight, or freeze. A fight response may manifest itself as arguing, defensiveness, yelling, or using inappropriate language. A flight response is not just leaving the situation, council, or school. Avoidance is also a flight response. When people become overwhelmed they freeze; they may come across as inactive or unable to make decisions. Fight, flight, and freeze are all stress responses. They are not intentional; rather, they are unconscious responses. The next charts illustrate how people know if they are not safe and what they do when they do not feel safe or welcomed.

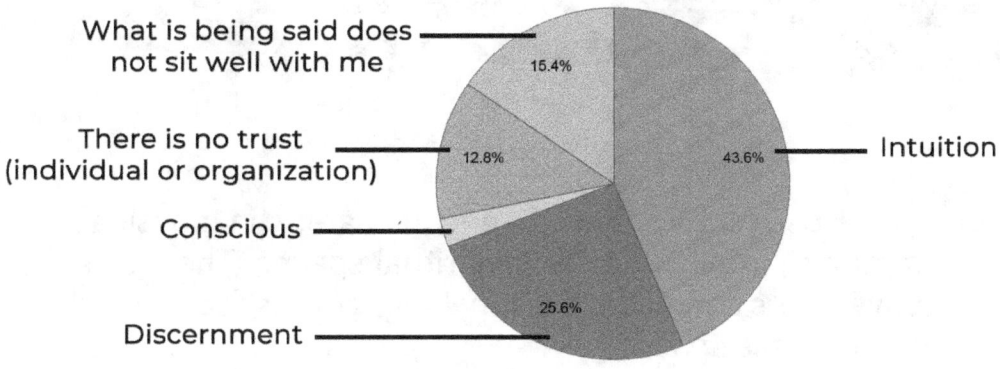

How people know when they are not safe.

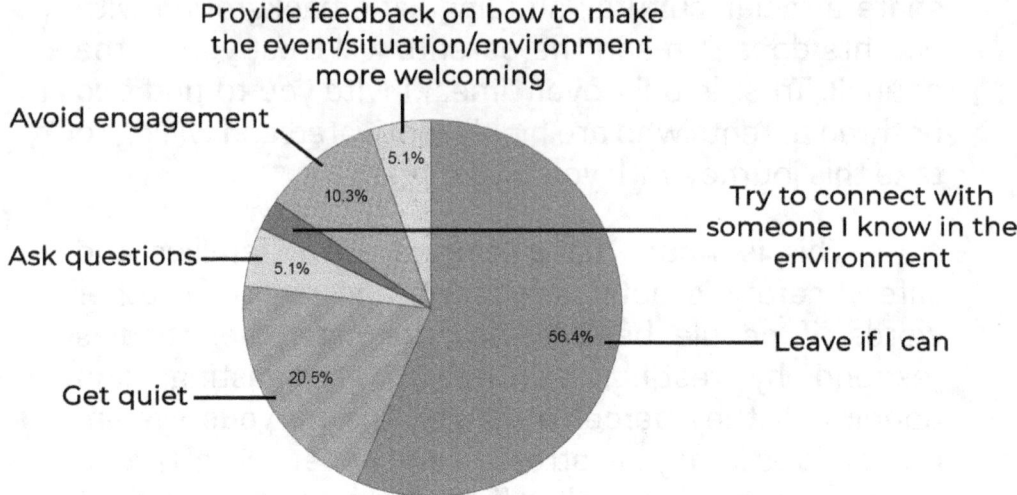

What people do when they don't feel safe or welcome.

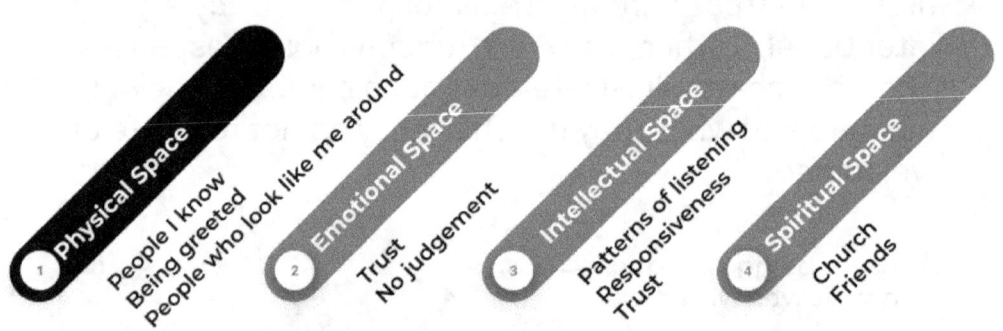

Hospitality seeks to ensure safety in physical, emotional, intellectual, and spiritual spaces. The figure above offers some ideas for making families feel safe in each of these spaces.

Guiding Frameworks

General Tips for Making Families Feel Safe

Physical Space

"Sometimes you want to go where everybody knows your name"

—Gary Portnoy

Be mindful about the structures, representations, and other aesthetics in the physical or virtual space. Black families are relational and social. Here are a few things to consider:

1. The design of the physical space
2. Greeting people (greeting them by name eventually)
3. Representation (images, leadership, music, lifeways, perspectives, experiences)
4. Making people feel connected

Design the physical space in ways that decentralize authority and instead promote socialization, bonding, and collaboration. On the next pages are some room-design diagrams that promote relationships and collaboration.

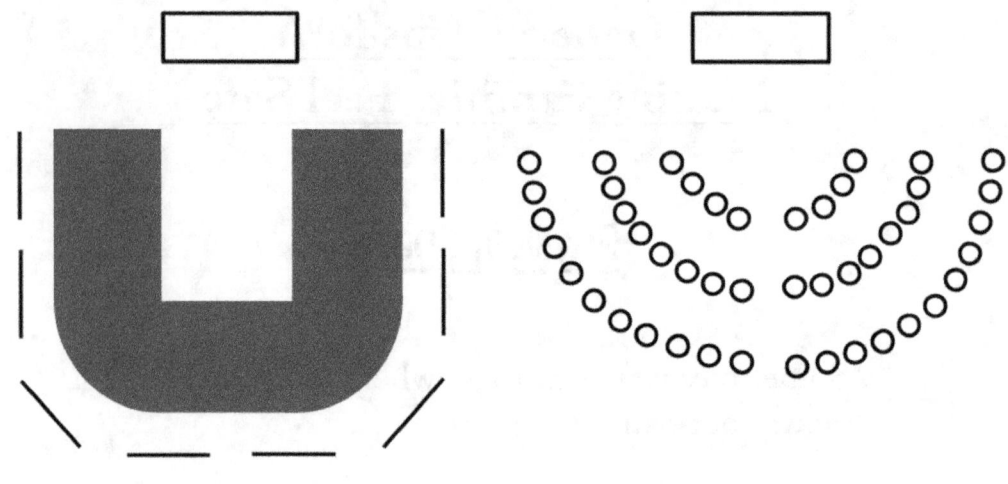

U-shape

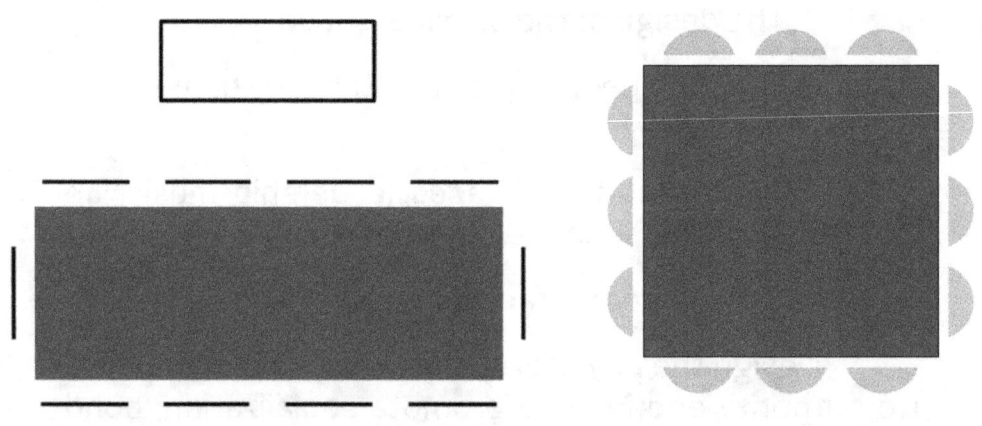

Board room

Banquet rounds

Loose Structure

Always make time for real connections. The physical or virtual space should be informal but structured. Agendas are great. Most people like to know what to expect. They need to know when the meeting will start and end, and the purpose of the meeting should always be included on the agenda. After the first one or two meetings, which give time for people to get used to attending and feeling out the space, the agenda should be shared with families two or three days prior (email or Google doc) for early access and review. Families should be given the opportunity to add topics to the agenda a few weeks prior to a gathering. The agenda is a guide. Things will come up and a Parking Lot is useful for documenting those things so people are heard. A Parking Lot is any method you use to capture the ideas, questions, and concerns without needing to pause the meeting to address them. They are items to be addressed at a later time or date. It is important that the information, shared in the Parking Lot, is responded to: "I did see that you wanted to discuss...and I want you to know that is on our agenda for next week," or "I did hear your concern and we will follow up with you to learn more about how we can support or hear you."

If it is not necessary for families to sign in, don't make them. The purpose of the sign-in should be to create a contact list. This list should be used for communicating and connecting. Another list can be created, as an option, for families to use to share information with one another. You would be amazed at the number of groups that meet on a regular basis and members do not have one another's contact information. This is a barrier to connectedness. A contact list should be an option.

Guest Speakers

It is wonderful to have guest speakers, but the majority of the time should not be for speakers. If speakers are a part of the curriculum, meet with the speakers prior to get an idea of what information they would like to share, and ask your families if they are interested in this information. I recommend creating a short form like the one in the appendix. Develop a process that enables guest speakers to have conversations with families about the information, and how it may be used to support their children or their capacity to support learning and wellness.

District Speakers

District speakers are people who work for the school district and have roles in teaching, learning, accountability, finances, hiring, etc. It is highly recommended that these speakers use a discussion format instead of merely sharing information. There needs to be a discussion about what the data means for Black students and, if the data are bleak, the actions being taken (SMART goals) to correct the situation. The council should collaborate to prepare constructive and critical questions for district presenters to discuss with the group. If the district speaker is not able to provide information about plans to improve services to students or is not seeking the advice of the council for implementation, the council should reconsider this type of interaction. It can be frustrating for families and takes time away from connecting and advocacy.

Greeting People

If there is a check-in table, create signs that are welcoming and provide direction on signing in or handouts needed. For the best results, have someone at the door to greet guests with a smile and by name. Information such as seating, name tags, restrooms, and so forth can be provided in other ways. It is important to learn people's names and faces and give them warm greetings.

Represent the people you are serving. Black families are looking for representation. It matters who greets them and who facilitates the work. The person leading this work does not need to be Black, but he or she needs to be able to center the lifeways, knowledge, practices, and values of Black people in every aspect of this work. This means the process of engagement and the content used to work with Black families must be representative of Black experiences, values, and preferences. Be mindful of the music and activities and be sure the work includes the concerns of Black families.

The Black experience in America has been one of struggle, joy, pain, love, and faith. Not all families have students who are struggling. Joy and hope are essential to this work. There must be a balance of problem-solving around issues, restoration of students and families, and opportunities to cultivate joy and love.

Areas where representation is needed in the council and in schools:

1. Leadership
2. Speakers
3. Ideas
4. Materials
5. Activities
6. Music
7. Aesthetics
8. Knowledge
9. Interactions
10. Processes for leading and following
11. Values
12. Cultural practices
13. Religious and spiritual considerations
14. Communication styles and preferences
15. Curriculum
16. Increasing joy for students and their families

Reflections

What makes you feel safe in a physical space?

How do you respond when you notice you are not safe or welcome in a space?

> "If we have a neuroception of safety, our nervous system wants to open, step closer, and engage"
>
> (Olson, 2014, p.17).

Emotional, Intellectual, and Spiritual Safety

Listening, responding, and demonstrating concern for the collective are all ways to make Black families feel safe. Listening and responding require the ability to withhold judgment. It is easy for this work to reinforce structural racism, Whiteness, and classism. How? Most of the people leading this work may be well-educated and middle-class. Many of us have assimilated in ways that perpetuate structural racism as a survival mechanism. As a result, there may be a lack of awareness of how things can be done to meet the same goals using different methods and approaches. Leaders of this work must create space to hear diverse perspectives and work collaboratively to use them. I invite leaders to develop skills that enable them to observe—not judge—to respond, and to become aware. To do this, leaders must first reflect on the ways they may perpetuate Whiteness and structural racism.

There are countless examples of Black children and youth who are excelling as integrated Black people. There are also countless examples of the strengths of Black families, and these examples are used to support the success of Black youth. We have been mis-educated to think such examples do not exist, but they can be found in books, in journals, in families, and in communities. This guide includes a recommended reading list on page 75, which you are invited to expand. It is also imperative to learn from churches, local communities,

Guiding Frameworks

and faith-based organizations and how to develop, build, and maintain trust with Black people. Bring those principles to the council and advocate for them in schools. Below are some ways in which you can grow internally and specific actions leaders can take to support Black children and youth.

Internal Development	External Actions
Develop congruence	Advocate for more alignment between what is said and what is done.
Identify triggers & traumas and heal	Advocate for learning opportunities around mindfulness, bias, microaggressions, patriarchy, and White supremacy.
Improve listening skills	Be a translator when there are miscommunications and misunderstandings. Insist that those working in schools develop their social-emotional skills.
Make sure people know you hear them	Advocate for minutes, notes, and written records that demonstrate patterns of concern.
Depersonalize reactions and responses (focus on the problems & issues)	Help others understand the dynamics at play (race, power, privilege, class, gender). Help people understand connections between historical atrocities and injustices and present inequities.
Learn what makes others feel safe enough to share, learn, and grow	Advocate for dual capacity-building around what makes students and Black families feel safe in schools.

Reflections

What makes you feel safe enough to share your ideas and observations?

How do you integrate your spirituality or faith into your life at work and at home?

Action

Based on what you have read in this section, identify three short, measurable, specific, realistic, and attainable goals for creating safe spaces for Black families.

1.

2.

3.

4

What's the Big Idea?!

Connections are important. Black students and their families have been isolated and disenfranchised from larger society due to structural racism and anti-Blackness. The BFAC can help correct this. Councils can make Black families feel safe by intentionally ensuring they are connected in schools. Start with ensuring people have opportunities to meet other people. Take it upon yourselves to create systems in which key people greet others by name and make personal introductions between guests/members.

Equally important is connecting your families to key people in schools and in the district. There is an assumption that everyone knows who to contact for what. Help familiarize Black families with important forms, processes, academic and behavioral standards, curricula, special programs, and direct services that would benefit their children. I was an active parent in a district for over four years before I knew the district had a Freedom School and before I learned how to access after-school programs. Are there people you know who are especially warm and knowledgeable? How may they assist in connecting Black families in schools? They may be parents, volunteers, or district personnel. Building their capacity to welcome Black families may be necessary. There are times in which a school's first family contact doesn't go as planned; school personnel may do things unintentionally that make families feel unwelcome. Talk to your families about what those things are and help build the capacity of the council leadership and school personnel to create safe spaces, making sure Black families are included. What makes one group feel safe does not necessarily make everyone feel safe and welcome.

Black families are social and political. The two cannot be separated. Black families want to discuss hard topics. They also want to share joy and celebrate accomplishments. Make space for all of it, even if the space must be outside of the regular gathering times. Think about social media, newsletters, members-only websites, or Yahoo groups that can be used to increase connections and share resources, joys, and concerns. Whenever you gather, plan to create space, even as little as 10 minutes, for socialization. You can create a structure in which refreshments are served 15 minutes prior to the meeting, or the meeting ends 10 minutes prior to the time you need to be out of a physical space; these structures make room for socialization. If someone comes to the meeting distraught, do not ignore that person. Have a plan in place for someone to speak with that person in private, take note of the person's concerns, bring the concerns to the larger group if given permission and if appropriate, and work to collectively support that individual.

What's the Big Idea?!

It is critical that people are given a telephone call or text if they have been attending and begin not to attend. A hospitality committee can be formed for this sort of outreach. If someone is sick, it is important that members from the group check in on them and see how they may support them. Celebrate or grieve as the community does. Demonstrating connection is important.

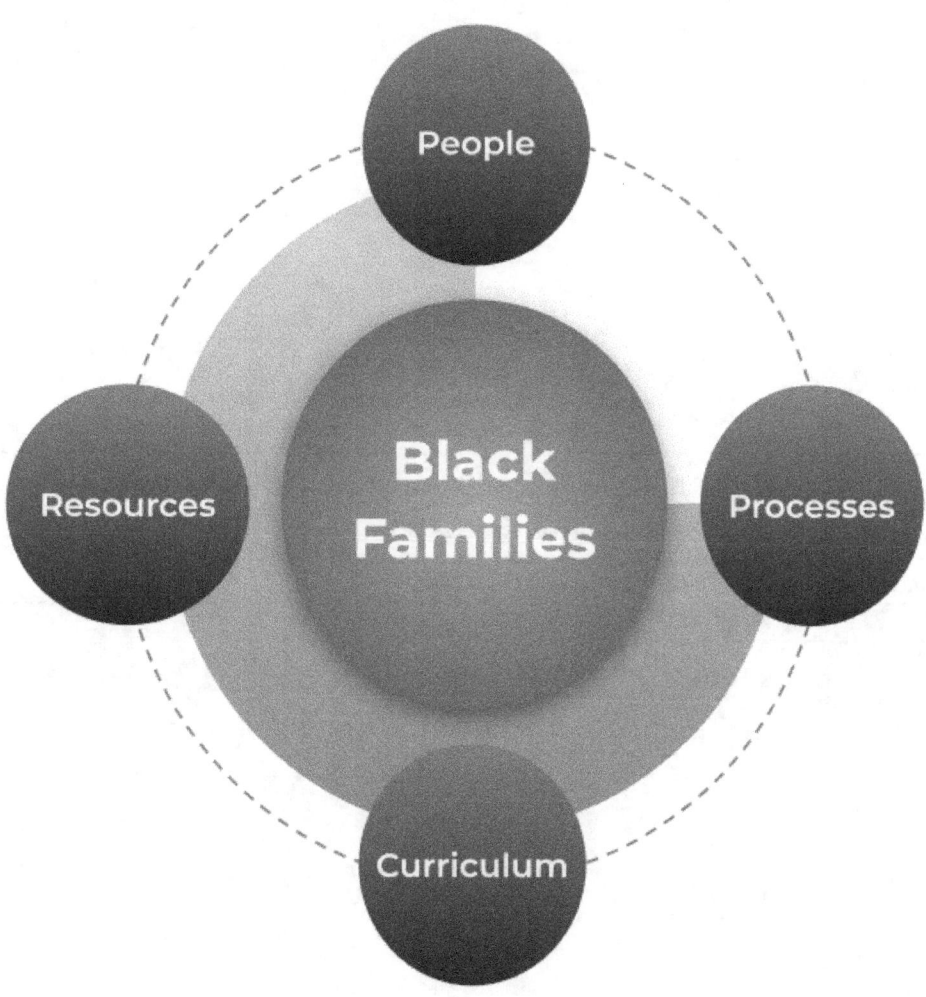

Ways to Connect Black Families in Schools

Reflections

Have you ever been part of a group? What actions did the group take to make you feel connected? Or what actions did you take to stay connected?

Have you ever been a part of a group and did not come around for a while? Did anyone reach out to you? If so, how? If not, how did that make you feel?

What's the Big Idea?!

What connections do you have that can benefit other families and Black students?

Action

Based on what you have read about connecting Black families in schools, what are three short, measurable, specific, and realistic goals for the council related to connections?

1.

2.

3.

5

Coming to an Agreement

There is power in agreement. It is important that this work is affirmative. Take time to develop group agreements about how members or guests are expected to interact and respond to one another. If everyone is to feel safe enough to share, create, and thrive there must be agreements to act in ways that are beneficial to students and families.

Here is a process for developing group agreements:

1. Ask the group to identify behaviors that would be important for creating a safe and collaborative environment.

2. Group the behaviors into themes (general concepts).

3. Narrow the themes down to ten, then four or five.

4. Create a graphic of the agreements (example on the next page) and use it in each meeting.

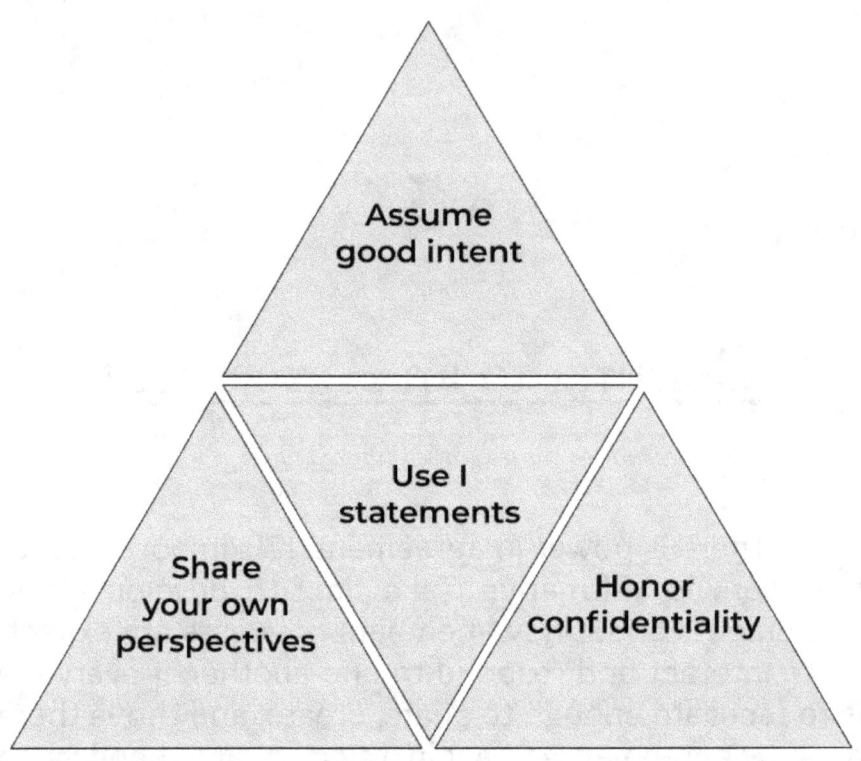
Sample Group Agreement Graphic

Once developed, the agreements should be reviewed by participants at each gathering. The agreements should be flexible and may change as needs change. Those leading this work should agree to be asset-based and collaborative, to listen, to be open to feedback, and to be willing to have courageous conversations.

Reflections

What behaviors do you believe are important to the success of the group?

How do you plan on modeling these behaviors?

Action

Based on what you have read about the importance of norms and agreements, identify two attainable and realistic goals for group agreements. Be sure to include target dates.

1.

2.

Coming to an Agreement

There needs to be conversations about White immunity, fragility, and emotionality. There also needs to be a discussion about internalized racism. There are resources and experts who can facilitate these discussions with your team. These resources may be found in many of your local universities, in professional organizations such as National Alliance of Black School Educators (NABSE), or California Association of Black School Educators (CABSE), or in resources, online and in print geared towards supporting diverse student success. Dr. Cheryl Matias is an expert on White Emotionality, and Dr. Nolan Cabreras is the leading expert on White Immunity.

If these topics are not brought to the surface, what will happen is people will show up and start to blame families for depressed student outcomes. Internalized racism may sound like: "These parents need to . . ." This statement is deficit-based and does not assume all parents want what is best for their children. A way to reframe such a statement is this: "I have noticed that some of our children have poor reading comprehension. Let's have a session on supporting reading comprehension." After such a suggestion is made, the council needs to work with school leaders to see what can be done in the classroom to support comprehension (or whatever learning issue was identified).

White fragility and emotionality may sound like: "I don't see race or color," or the person may become very defensive or start to cry when there are discussions about race and Black people share their experiences. When this happens, all the attention is likely to shift to avoid conversations that may make "mixed company" uncomfortable. This work is focused on making Black families feel safe. Others are welcome to join, but they are not the focus of this work. This work requires courageous conversations and the experiences and knowledge of Black people is centered in this work.

Equitable By Design

6

District-Level Advisory Councils

The advisory council seeks to work collaboratively with districts. There are several ways the district can partner with Black family councils: help in obtaining board approval; provide school leadership training; develop capacity-building around Black parent engagement; supply meeting space, access to virtual platforms, staff support for meetings, advertisement, child care, refreshments; and seek BFAC advisement about things that impact Black scholars.

Purpose

The purpose of a district advisory council is to develop a centralized and collective voice for students. This group provides vision, direction, and support to the district and school sites for matters concerning the academic and social-emotional wellness of students. The district advisory is a hub for resources, advocacy, and support that feed into district initiatives and school sites. Representatives from several schools make up the membership of the district advisory whereas membership in school site advisories includes, but is not limited to, district advisory members. For example, Co-Chairs of school site BFACs are members of the district advisory. They attend district advisory meetings in order to develop goals, locate resources, and work strategically on behalf of families and students.

Priorities and Goals

A small group, including community members, parents, district leaders, and current or former principals, needs to develop a set of guiding priorities and clear goals related to Black student achievement. This process takes weeks, even months.

Board Approval

The parent advisory group, or those interested in forming one, should identify one or two board members who would support the work of the Black Family Advisory Council. It is a good idea to have principals, current or former, as proponents for the work as well. Including principals is purposeful because they bring another perspective and insight that is useful for developing and sustaining a strong council. Use the priorities and goals developed by the small group and the district data to prepare a presentation for the Board on why the Black family council will be beneficial and how the advice of the council will bolster the work that needs to be done with Black students. Ask to be recognized as a council that will advise on things concerning Black children.

Things to consider for a board presentation:

1. Who are the people who can support this work?
2. How can we connect this work to what schools do or need to do?
3. What are our priorities and how do they align with the students' and schools' needs?
4. Who is the person with the most accurate school data?
5. Who are the people and organizations (churches, after-school programs, colleges, Black Greeks, parent groups) that can support us during our presentation to the board?
6. Who can explain the data?
7. Who can co-construct the presentation?
8. Who should be a part of the board presentation?
9. What are the opportunities for advice from the council to the district/schools?

Reflections

Who are the people who can support this work?

What data can be used to support a board presentation?

Who can work with you to get the data in an understandable format?

Action

Based on what you have read about presentation to the board, identify three short, specific, measurable, and attainable goals for a presentation to the board. Include a timeline, roles, and responsibilities.

1.

2.

3.

7

Advisement

"When you develop a supportive school and classroom culture that places a priority on relationships, you begin to lay the foundation for lowering anxiety and opening the neural pathways of learning"

(Olson, 2014, p. 102).

Sometimes we do not know where to start. What should you advise on? Below are five starting points that have shown to be effective in supporting Black student academic success and well-being, when guided and advised by a family council:

Important Areas for Advisement:

1	**Representation**	▶ Curriculum
		▶ Education Models/Leadership
		▶ School Practices

2	Instruction	▶ Culturally Informed Practices
		▶ Making Students Feel Capable
		▶ High Expectations and High Support
3	Safety	▶ Physical Spaces
		▶ Emotional and Intellectual Safety
		▶ Making Students Feel Valued
4	School Culture	▶ Welcoming Spaces
		▶ Evidence-Based Teaching Practices that Support Black Students
5	Literacy	▶ High Interest Readings & Topics
		▶ Home-School Connections
		▶ A Focus on Mastery and Vocabulary
		▶ Racial Literacy

Reflections

Does anyone on the team have expertise in any of these areas? If not, do they know people who do?

Advisement

> **Are there teachers and district resources we can partner with around these areas so we are informed and strategic?**

Action

Based on what you have learned in this section, what are three short, measurable, realistic, and attainable goals the council can set for areas of advice to the district and schools?

1.

2.

3.

Structure

It is important that the advisory has some structure. Create a 1-page document detailing the mission, vision, priorities, and goals of the council. A sample is provided on the website www.bridgesleadership.com. Detail the district council's organizational structure in a set of bylaws. Decide what types of positions there will be and how they will function within the organization, district, and schools. Will there be a chair, secretary, and members? Who are the members? Your bylaws will take time to develop. I have a sample on my website for you (www.bridgesleadership.com). Bylaws are best co-constructed by a team of people over a specific period of time. Families must be part of this process. Perspectives that represent an array of Black experiences would strengthen the work. It is important that all roles be clarified with job descriptions.

Your document should detail how people are placed into positions, length of terms, and conditions for those terms and positions. Develop a process for replacing positions should there be a need for change or a vacancy. In the beginning stages, co-chairs are strongly recommended. You may choose to align the structure of the organization with other parent organizations in the district such as district English language parent advisory or parents of students with disabilities advisory councils. This work is not parallel to the work of PTA, and alignments with such groups are discouraged. Earlier we discussed being loosely structured. Establishing 2-year terms during the initial phases of the council provides consistency. An example of an organizational chart is given below.

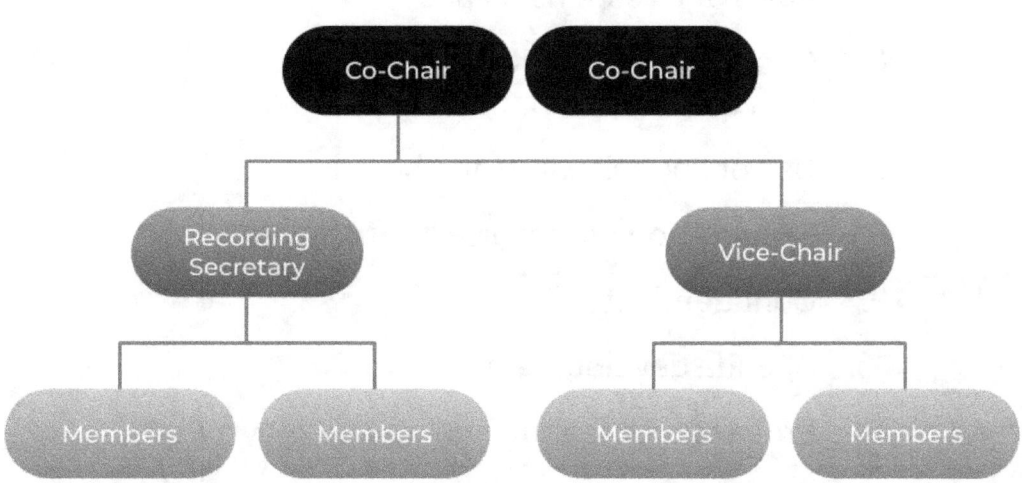

<u>Policies</u>

Outline in writing how you expect to do things. Policies should be flexible and change as needed. A process must be spelled out at the beginning for making changes when they become necessary. Policy guides practice. Everything does not need a policy; however, if there are specific areas that are prone to conflicts and miscommunication, a policy is necessary. You might start by reviewing the policies of the district language learner parent advisory or special education parent advisory councils. Those documents are publicly accessible and may be useful in guiding how the council can create policies. Below I have provided a few areas for policy consideration.

Areas for Policy Consideration

1. Voting
2. Council leadership roles and terms
3. Decision-making
4. Guest speakers
5. Roles and responsibilities
6. Communication within the council, in schools, and with district personnel
7. Use of council name and brand
8. Expectations to resolve internal conflict
9. Confidentiality
10. Agenda development
11. Process for creating and updating bylaws
12. Process for removal from leadership
13. District personnel participation in council meetings
14. Leadership development and capacity building

8

Capacity Building

It is highly recommended that the BFAC leaders (parents, families, and community members) engage in on-going leadership development and capacity building and that this be an integral part of the structure of the organization. Some suggested areas in which capacity should be built are: healing-centered practices; site councils; Local Control and Accountability Plan (LCAP); reading and understanding data; universal design for learning; facilitating meetings; team-building; managing conflict; evidence-based practices for Black student achievement; and culturally informed mindfulness or other contemplative practices.

Radiate Joy

In an effort to model and radiate the change we want to be, I invite leaders to think about their own mindfulness, starting with self-care. I want leaders of this work to commit to increasing their joy and happiness. When we engage in particular activities we increase our body's store of dopamine, oxytocin, serotonin, and endorphins. Dopamine sends transmitters to the brain that signal pleasure. It is also useful for thinking and planning (De Neve, 2011; Grosberg et al., 2012). Serotonin stabilizes mood and gives a sense of well-being. It also helps with sleeping, eating, and digestion. Oxytocin helps with bonding, and endorphins are chemicals that alleviate pain and stress. These are all beneficial to us and aid in our work. Here are some of the ways I increase my joy and happiness along with the good chemicals associated with them:

Dopamine	Oxytocin
1. Identify goals and tasks and complete them 2. Foot soaks 3. Massages 4. Facials 5. Yoga 6. Long walks 7. My favorite foods or drinks 8. Celebrate small wins	1. Spend time with my favorite people 2. Hug 3. Give compliments or encourage others 4. Volunteer 5. Give gifts or cards 6. Express gratitude 7. Read or listen to something inspirational
Serotonin	**Endorphins**
1. Prayer 2. Guided meditation 3. Time in the sun 4. Be in nature 5. Breath work 6. Qigong 7. Short brisk walks	1. Laugh 2. Essential oils 3. Dark chocolate 4. Music 5. Dance 6. Exercise

Let joy and happiness help you in this work. They are contagious. They will help to ensure service is coming from a place of fullness and not depletion. You are also invited to increase your rest, exercise, time with people who energize you, service to others, and daily doses of gratitude. Once we embody these practices, we can invite our Black families and students to join us.

Reflections

What are you already doing each day that energizes you or increases your joy?

Have you completed an energy profile that indicates whether you prefer to be outdoors or indoors or if certain scents inspire you?

Who are the people who inspire you when you are with them? Who do you inspire or encourage?

Capacity Building

Action

Based on what you read in this section, what are three specific, realistic, and measurable ways you can increase your daily doses of joy and happiness?

1.

2.

3.

What is your plan for an extremely hectic day?

A part of the council's work can be around building capacity to engage in advocating for and supporting the growth and development of Black scholars. Identify shared readings, podcasts, and videos that can enhance the council's cognition and capability to advocate for and support scholars in the following areas: universal design for learning; culturally responsive pedagogies; differentiated instruction; African-centered teaching and learning strategies; healing-centered practices; critical mentoring, racial socialization; mental health; critical race theory; validation theory; and suicide prevention.

Suggested Readings

1. *Learning While Black*, Janice E Hale
2. *There is Nothing Wrong with Black Students*, J. Kunjufu
3. *Cultivating Genius*, Gholdy Muhammed
4. *200 Educational Strategies to Teach Students of Color*, J. Kunjufu
5. *Research in Parental Involvement: Strategies for Education and Psychology*, Yvette Latunde
6. Any books about Black Gifted Children
7. *Culturally Responsive School Leadership*, Muhammed Khalifa
8. *Education in Movement Spaces*, Django Paris
9. *Hope Quotient*, Ray Johnston
10. *Culturally Responsive Teaching and the Brain*, Zaretta Hammond
11. *The Abundant Community*, John McKnight, Peter Block

Reflections

Think about schools that are successful with Black students. What is happening there?

What practical steps can you take to learn more about what works to support the academic success and well-being of Black students (all incomes, abilities, mixed-race, languages)?

Capacity Building

Action

Based on what you just read, list three goals for increasing your capacity to support Black students' academic success and overall well-being inside and outside of schools. Be sure the goals are measurable, attainable, realistic, and have a timeline.

1.

2.

3.

Equitable By Design

9

Yearly Practice Ideas

"Of all of the policy changes necessary to reactivate our community life and the care of our democratic society, redefining the uses of time is most important and most difficult"

(McKnight et al, 2012, p. 106).

Let me recommend some activities that will build the council's capacity to support the success and well-being of Black students:

- ▶ Analyze and review district data, strategic planning, LCAP and site plan reviews.
- ▶ Develop a yearly calendar.
- ▶ Develop one or two new strategic community partnerships.
- ▶ Meet with district leadership around specific goals and priorities.
- ▶ Update site leader toolkit.
- ▶ Use healing-centered practices with families and scholars.

The council is NOT limited to working around the data the school has made a priority. The council can work to develop goals or advise on things outside of school data that represent their values and priorities for their children. For example, the council may consider exposure to non-traditional careers, mental health, ethics, mentoring, and increased psychological safety in schools.

Reflective questions about data:

- What is the school/district doing to disrupt the narrative of Black students as the lowest performing group?
- Are there areas where students are excelling, such as science?
- What is different about the standards in different subjects and how are different subjects being taught to students?
- What evidence-based practices is the district using to specifically target Black students in areas in which they are underserved?
- Are there experts who can help build the capacity of teachers to better support Black students in the classroom?

Ask that school data regarding Black students be provided to the council using plain language and graphics. Ask that someone come to explain what the data means for language arts, science, and math. Ask that the data be prepared for the current year, pre-Common Core, and after the implementation of Common Core. Having this data ensures that we have accurate information. Ask to review the school data regarding discipline by race and school site. Interpreting the data gets tricky because the terms "expulsion" and "suspension" are specific in schools. Schools are now being very creative in delivering harsh discipline. Look for discipline data by race and gender. Then ask to see the number of students sent to local charter or alternative schools by race and gender.

Site Plans

> Education as the practice of freedom affirms healthy self esteem in students as it promotes their capacity to be aware and live consciously. It teaches them to reflect and act in ways that further self-actualization, rather than conformity to the status quo
>
> (bell hooks, *Teaching Community: A Pedagogy of Hope*).

Each school is required to have a school site plan. It is the school's plan of action for raising the achievement of students and improving educational programming. Each school submits its plan to the district for review. The BFAC should be a part of both the school's and the district's review process for the site plan. When you review the site plan, you are looking for targeted strategies, resources, and support for Black students and for students who are underperforming. These two groups are not necessarily the same students. Black students overall need an increased sense of safety and belonging in schools regardless of their school/academic performance, and efforts toward that need to be in the site plan.

We can assume that structural racism has been harmful whether or not we see the evidence in children and youths' behavior(s) or academic performance. How can healing-centered practices be used with students now? What would that look like? How are schools working to demonstrate care and value for Black students? How can the council help guide this? The school site plan is one area in which these foci can become goals and be measured. Black students need and deserve evidence-based practices.

These are the practices found in schools with no racial, ability, gender, or economic gaps[5]:

- Teaching: Students are made to feel valued and capable. There is a focus on understanding and mastery. Clarity is promoted. Teaching is culturally, socially, and personally responsive. Teachers check for understanding, provide feedback, and adapt. Guided practice is promoted and fluency is built with gatekeeper vocabulary.

- Leadership: Leaders influence desire to change. Leaders influence belief in the capacity to improve and succeed. Leaders influence clarity about roles and responsibility and build capacity to succeed.

- Healing-Centered Practices: Music & movement (discharging negative energy or celebrating), art, dance, breath-work, yoga, meditation, prayer, sharing are embedded into the work.

---

[5] Source: National Center for Urban School Transformation, https://ncust.com/leadership-in-americas-best-urban-schools/

Promising Practices

- Co-constructing what is measured in schools
- Co-constructing family engagement initiatives
- Co-researching problems of practice, identifying solutions, implementing solutions, measuring success, and re-designing
- Collectively identifying culturally sustaining curricula
- Co-designing concrete ways to center racial equity in all subjects and disciplines
- Co-creating standards for family engagement
- Embedding opportunities for student voices to be used in teachers' and school leaders' evaluations

Reflections

Has anyone attended a school site council training? If not, when will someone be attending?

What are practical ways healing-centered activities can be embedded into this work with families and students?

Action

Based on what you have learned in this section (I know, that was a lot of information!), identify three short, measurable, attainable, and realistic goals for yearly practices.

1.

2.

3.

Relationships are important. One of the goals of the district Black Family Advisory Council should be to develop relationships within the district and between schools. This can be accomplished by strategically ensuring that the leadership participates in district-sponsored learning opportunities. Some of those opportunities are training for parent leaders, school site councils, and Local Control and Accountability Plan (LCAP). The same person need not attend everything, but rather several people can take turns engaging in learning opportunities and preparing some information that could be shared with the larger group. At the end of the learning opportunities, the council can engage in dialogue that considers how that information may be used to support Black students and families and if the information shared can be enhanced in ways that resonate more with evidence on working with Black families.

Some things to think about after attending trainings:

1. Did you feel welcome?
2. If not, what would have made you feel more welcome?
3. How did the process of teaching resonate with you, and how would it resonate with other families?
4. Was the information shared in ways that encouraged questions and interaction or was the learning passive?
5. Is the information useful in supporting Black students? If not, what would have made it more useful?
6. What would be the best ways to share this information with all types of families?

Reflections

Who are the people at our school site who would support this work?

How can the council partner with the families of children with special needs, language learners, Advancement Via Individual Determination (AVID), and the Black Student Union?

Are there PTA members who could also support this work?

Action

Based on what you have learned in this section, identify three short, measurable, realistic, and attainable goals for relationships within schools. Be sure to develop a timeline for implementation.

1.

2.

3.

What local businesses and organizations can we partner with to support Black students?

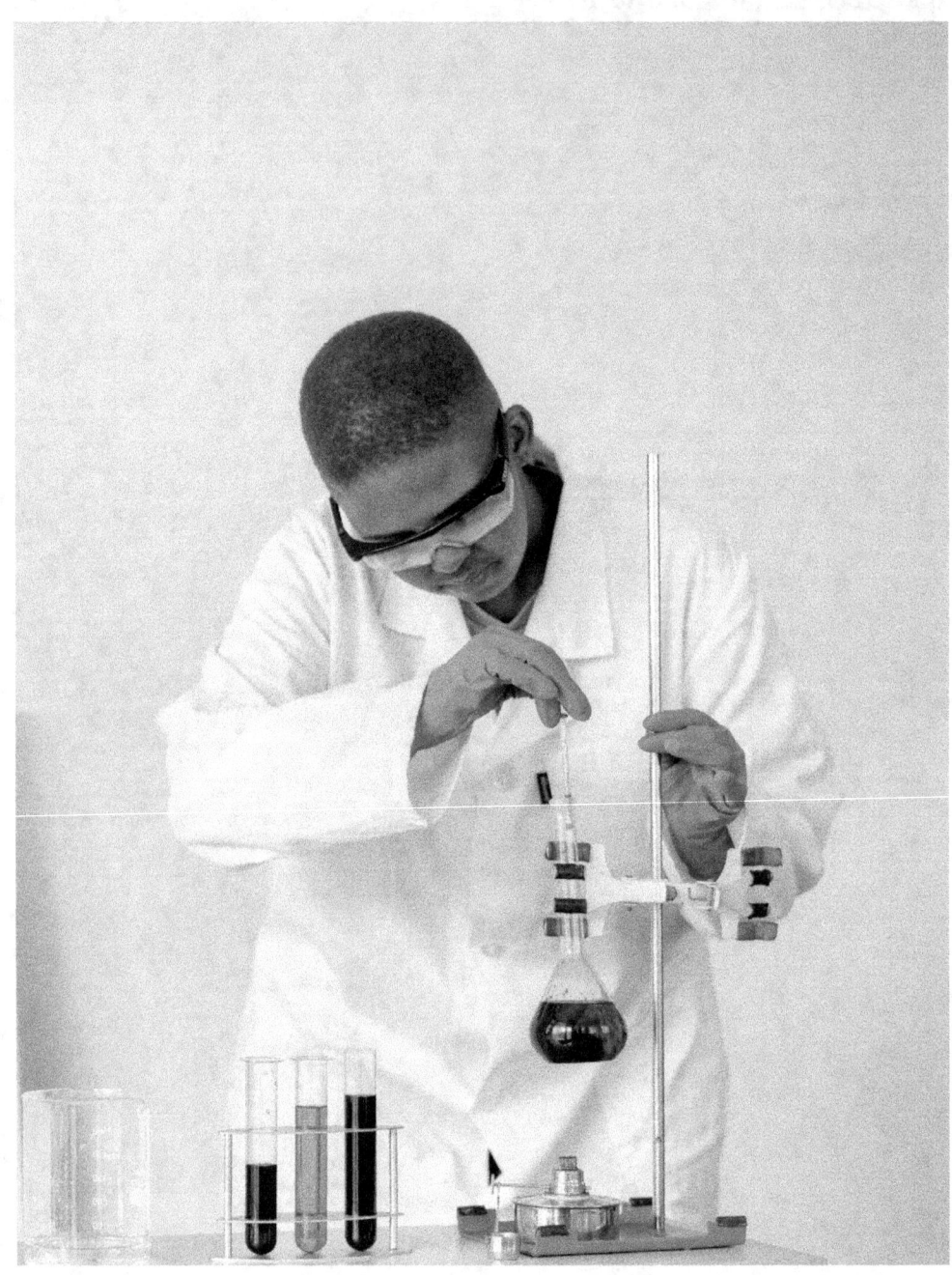

10

Monthly Experiences

"Building community is more than occasional, tangible events like holding picnics, constructing a park, or doing a group service project. It involves the more fundamental task of rearing a child, promoting health, and keeping the streets safe"

(McKnight et al., 2012, p. 67).

Several things are important for the council to think about, but the most important aspect is students' success and well-being. Student success involves both academic and non-academic aspects. The academics are clear: math, language arts, and geography. What is not as clear is that non-academic factors inhibit or facilitate learning. All are important to learning.

Factors that influence learning:

Non-academic	Academic
Feeling safe (emotionally, physically, spiritually, psychologically)	Thinking preferences

Non-academic	Academic
Feeling cared for	Pedagogy
Feeling capable	High expectations of students and high student support
High expectations	Connections to culture, backgrounds, and experiences
Involvement in extracurricular activities	Classroom structure
A belief the teacher likes you	Teaching and learning fit
Self-regulation	A focus on mastery
Individual personality	Vocabulary
Strengths – academic confidence	School culture
Interests	School leadership practices
Family background and experiences	Use of plain language to communicate standards
Economic stability	Collaboration between professionals
Communication styles and preferences	Making students feel capable
General health	Tutoring
Social integration in school and neighborhood	Metacognition
Stress, anxiety	Specific learning strategies

Monthly Meetings

Each month the district advisory meets with district leadership to advance Black student success. The council should have clear goals and clear contacts for meeting those goals. For example, if the goal is advocacy for equitable funding for academic and social interventions, who would be the person at the district level responsible for those topics? It is imperative that you, as district leaders, have met as a council and developed a thoughtful plan for interacting with other district leaders. You also want to make sure what you advise is supported with evidence (from the literature) and demonstrated to work with Black students or families. For example, there are some "best" and "evidence-based" practices that have been "proven" to work, but not with African American or Black students and families.

Below is an example of an evidence-based (dual capacity-building, hospitality, and math) initiative for promoting math success for Black students.

Goal: Increase Black students' success in advanced math as assessed by summative tests, projects, and overall performance.

School Leaders

Support teachers, school counselors, and families in increasing their capacity to focus on mastery and key vocabulary in advanced math courses.

Teachers

Priority 1: Increase teachers' capacity to connect with students' background, culture, and interests.

Context: Teachers can choose where to start (culture, background, interests). Teachers work with school leaders to decide the best progress monitoring tools.

Priority 2: Increase teachers' capacity to focus on mastery.

Context: Teachers work with school leaders to determine a baseline and beginning areas.

Counselors

School counselors will increase their capacity to apply validation theory and hospitality to Black students. Using multiple forms of data, the counselors will work to (1) identify students for advanced math courses and (2) connect students and their families to people and direct resources that will foster success in advanced math.

Counselors will provide on-going emotional, social, and academic support for Black students using concepts of validation theory. Some of those practices include:

- Learning students' names
- Giving students opportunities to witness themselves as successful learners
- Ensuring that the curriculum reflects or connects to the students' backgrounds and interests
- Sharing knowledge and inviting students to opportunities
- Telling students, "You can do this and I am going to help you."
- Working with coaches and teachers to help students select courses and plan their futures

- Helping students connect with one another; creating those opportunities
- Serving as mentors for students and making an effort to meet with them outside of class such as in patio areas, cafeterias, and/or the library.

Families

The council will work through schools and councils to increase family members' capacity to focus on mastery and reinforce important vocabulary outside of schools. Families can choose if they want to learn:

- Specific math learning strategies
- How to reinforce math mastery
- About specific resources that can support their children directly
- Strategies to reduce math anxiety

Reflections

What are non-academic factors that have benefited you in your life?

Who were the people who made a positive difference in your life as a child/youth?

11

Messaging

A council's messaging is important. I use the term messaging instead of marketing intentionally. The council is not selling anything. There is no special recipe for family engagement. The council works when it is supported and when people working in it focus on the right things. It is important that the messaging about the council is clear. The council is a support for parents of Black and African American children. It is focused on collaborative partnerships that advocate supporting Black students. Some of the ways it accomplishes its purpose are by building capacity; partnering with the community and schools; and empowering families with resources, information, and connections. The message needs to be: "Anyone interested in the success of Black students is welcome to participate." Families lead the work.

In order for the messaging to be clear, it is important that individuals do not speak on behalf of the council without a consensus and conversation.

The district webpage can be used to share meeting announcements, agendas, and minutes. The council is not obligated to make minutes publicly accessible in the same way that school-mandated groups like school site councils are. District email blasts can be used to remind families of meetings. Great success has been found in working with Black churches and other churches, mosques, and synagogues; after-school programs; school counselors; and sports programs to share information about meetings or programs. These community partners are vital.

Clear agendas help with meeting messaging whereas websites, blogs, and social media pages can communicate who makes up the council and what it does. It is important that the messaging is consistent and that there is a strategy for messaging. A council can be in existence for years and yet people do not know about it. How does that happen? It happens when the council works in isolation from the larger community. It is important to focus on Black students while being engaged with the broader community and the schools within the district.

Reflections

What do you want people to understand about the council?

Messaging

> **How can the council ensure that the message is clear and consistent?**

Invitations are important. Phone calls and emails are still the best ways to make initial contacts with families. This first contact will set the tone. The contact should be warm, specific, and brief. Texts may be useful reminders after rapport and purpose for the gatherings have been established. The invitation starts with a call or email but ends with the event. Coffees, mixers, and other informal gatherings have been successful in initially gathering those interested in the success of Black students and families. The person making the invite matters. Families trust their faith-based institutions and other parents. They also want to hear from teachers. After-school and sports programs, Black student unions, Black teacher associations, Black administrator groups, parent groups like Mocha Moms, and school counselors are also good partners in reaching families.

Reflections

How do you like to be invited to things?

Does it matter who invites you? If so, why? If not, why?

Messaging

Action

Based on what you already know and what you've read, what are three ways to invite Black families to the council? Be sure to pay attention to tone, method, and messaging.

1.

2.

3.

Equitable By Design

12

Recognizing and Using Strengths

> We are enough: Making the shift requires that we act as if each of us and all of us have all that is needed. We have the gifts, the structures, and the capabilities needed now. We have the capacities in our families and communities
>
> (McKnight et al., 2012, p. 116).

It is important that the council learn about the strengths and unique skills of the leaders and members. It will be important that those strengths are highlighted and strategically utilized over time to benefit the council and, ultimately, students. You can learn peoples' strengths by:

- ▶ A simple inventory (online)
- ▶ A google survey
- ▶ Taking time to listen to people talk about their unique strengths and perspectives (someone should be mindful to capture those notes)
- ▶ Focus groups (audio record, take notes, ask clarifying or further questions)

A few strengths that are especially needed in this work are marketing, public relations, education, and community organization. The council needs: people connected authentically in the community; people who make other people feel seen; great listeners; people with negotiation skills; artists; musicians; storytellers; and great meeting facilitators.

Reflections

How do you feel when people recognize your strengths and unique perspectives?

Recognizing and Using Strengths

What are ways to recognize everyone's strengths over time?

Action

Based on what you have just read, what are three ways the council can identify, recognize, and use the strengths of leaders and members in this work? Be sure the goals are measurable and attainable.

1.

2.

3.

13

Interactive and Interdependent Work

The families that come to this work are diverse. There should be intentionality in creating gatherings that are interactive and developmental. People like to spend time wisely. No one wants to come and be a passive learner. If there is a speaker, allow for questions and a follow-up conversation about how the information may be used. Prior to an event with speakers, allow members to give input into what aspects of the topic they want to know. We strongly recommend that meetings mainly be for working groups that will collaborate on strategy or work to solve issues. It is more effective to establish groups that can work on specific priorities than to come to a meeting to discuss issues with no time for researching and creating a plan to solve those issues. Some issues may require additional resources and time, and those are great opportunities for working groups to apply their skills. It is important that those groups are given ample time to address specific issues and bring solutions to the larger group for consensus.

All of this takes time. One of the biggest mistakes a council can make is over scheduling a meeting. It is better to have more time to dialogue, create, and solve than to have one-way communication and information sharing. Remember, "talking at" rather than "working with" is what is often done to Black parents in other areas of the educational system. It is not effective. It does not recognize families as thinking and intuitive. Parents have all sorts of experience and knowledge. Although we do not want to make the gathering so academic that people feel they need advanced degrees to understand what is discussed, at the same time, the council and its members as a whole should build their capacity in the following areas:

- ▶ How the education system works
- ▶ Evidence-based practices for Black students
- ▶ How to make students feel safe
- ▶ How to negotiate with teachers and staff
- ▶ How to make Black families feel safe to fully participate in schools

By building capacity in these areas, we make the gatherings relational, collective, interactive, developmental, hospitable, and linked to learning.

I cannot say this enough: as soon as you realize you have offended someone, apologize immediately. Forgiveness and grace make the council work. Leaders of this work have to develop themselves as leaders. The council is operating in a system that has not centered Black people, and so there is tension and angst. This work is countercultural, and even those we aim to support may fight it. This work may be misunderstood. People who want solutions often want them now, but this work takes time.

Below I have tried to conceptualize a realistic timeframe for a new Advisory Council.

1	Identify a small group of interested participants	**2-4 months**
2	Develop goals, priorities, mission, structure	**4-6 months**
3	Make a Board presentation	**6-8 months after initial meetings**
4	Launch event for larger community	**6-12 months**
5	Revisit district-level council structure	**6-12 months**
6	Form bylaws/structure	**6-12 months**
7	Begin school-site advisory councils	**12-24 months**

Reflections

Where are you on this journey?

What barriers do you anticipate?

How much time do you think you will need to get started? Or when do you plan to start the process, and why is that timing appropriate?

Interactive and Interdependent Work

Action

Based on what you are learning, what are two specific and measurable goals for launching or expanding your council? Be sure to include target dates.

1.

2.

Things You May Need

When you do not have confidence and you feel separated or threatened, you are unable to be hospitable. When you have a life in a connected and confident community, it is welcoming; hospitality is generated because people feel so good about themselves that they want others to share it

(McKnight et al., 2012, p. 78).

This work is not solely about monetary resources. Things to consider in addition to the use of parental involvement funds are space, childcare, and meeting settings. Some of the things you may need together with ideas for developing them are below.

Healing-centered Practices

- Begin gatherings with opportunities to move, then add grounding activities (sensing, breath-work) (5 minutes).
- Use ice breaker activities to promote team-building and trust.
- Prioritize connections over agendas and products.
- Encourage story-telling during gatherings; it promotes bonding.
- Discharging activities remove negative energy from your body: shaking, clapping, stomping, dancing, tapping, Qigong, walking, and running.
- Grounding: Breath-work, Qigong, sensing activities.
- Encourage all leaders to develop a self-care routine. Check in.

Space

There should be enough space for people to be comfortable. The space should be set up in ways that promote connections, relationships, and learning. Be aware of aesthetics.

If there are sites with low attendance (attendance is a tertiary, not a primary, concern), share space. There is nothing that says multiple schools cannot share space for meetings and learning opportunities.

Setting

Families can meet at the school site or a neutral place such as a community center, a space on a school or district campus designated for families, or a local church. Churches and community centers are often perceived to be safer than schools.

Virtual Meetings

Music, attention to the aesthetics of the presenters' backgrounds, time sharing the screen, and the use of breakout rooms are very important.

- Allow people to choose the rooms unless there are specific groups that need to be together.
- Do not record meetings without asking for group permission prior.
- Open the space 5-7 minutes prior to the meeting to allow for rapport building and connections.

- Use music as people wait for the meeting to start. I have provided a playlist for you. One set to remind members of the purpose of BFAC, and the other to open meetings, and for mind-body practice.
- Stay after the meeting (end on time) in case there are questions.
- Encourage people to connect via direct chat with one another.
- Still share norms.
- Still use a Parking Lot for additional questions.
- To make meetings interactive use Jamboard (Google), Padlet, Google slides, and breakout rooms.

Childcare/direct services to children and youth

Councils may partner with districts and school sites to provide care, tutoring, or supervision during meetings. Most districts already have these resources. The council may advise how they would like these services to reflect the cultural values of the group. The time with youth can be used for literature, for cultural activities, to develop learning strategies, to play or for help with homework.

Messaging

Partner to get the word out about the council. Churches, after-school programs, coaches, clubs, Black Student Unions, NAACP, PTA are some of the venues that are useful in sharing the message about the good work the council will do.

If the district council also has school-based site leaders and members, be sure to align goals, share resources, and provide support for those sites. It is important that there are shared district-level gatherings that include site leaders. Meeting regularly, virtually, or in person to discuss successes and challenges will benefit the entire organization. The monthly gatherings are a time for socialization, planning, and problem solving; it is important to have a balance of these. Gatherings should focus on the organization's goals and priorities, but these cannot be separated from the social, political, spiritual, and moral concerns of members. Leadership in this space should be decentralized and fluid.

Meetings

"The purpose of a democracy is to provide the opportunity for citizens to create abundant communities"

(McKnight et al., 2012, p. 109).

This work has a rhythm; it may take time to find what that is. Try to plan a yearly calendar that considers the district calendar. You want to increase the likelihood people can attend by avoiding too many calendar conflicts. There is no perfect time. We have found alternating times (morning and evening) may work, but a regular time is recommended. Ask families and community members for the best days and times. A word of caution: this work is to be inclusive of all incomes, backgrounds, and experiences. We must be careful not to make this work classist. We cannot structure this work to be accessible exclusively to middle-class and highly educated folks. This is why we need to be so closely connected to the community and listen so that we are responsive to community needs and desires.

Meetings are not a sign of progress. Progress is a sign of progress.

In preparing for meetings, consider:

- ▶ Invitations (How far in advance do you need to share the invitation?)
- ▶ Messaging (What is your message?)
- ▶ Collaborating across campuses (How can you communicate that this is collective work?)
- ▶ Agenda (Did you open the agenda to allow for the input of the families and the community?)
- ▶ Meaningful engagement (What are you asking families to do besides attend a meeting?)

Meaningful Engagement

What is happening? What is true (data/stories/patterns)? What is needed? What is helpful? What is possible? Find out what is happening with Black families and Black scholars from the perspectives of students, families, communities, and educators. What data can be used to substantiate what is happening? Look at literature on whatever topic is under consideration. Use the data, literature, and experts to identify what would be helpful. Develop strategic partnerships to determine what is possible to design and deliver for Black families and scholars.

Interactive and Interdependent Work

Action

Based on what you are learning, what are three specific, realistic, and measurable goals for meetings and meaningful engagement opportunities? Be sure to include target dates.

1.

2.

3.

"Whether we're talking about race or gender or class, popular culture is where the pedagogy is, it's where the learning is."

— bell hooks

Strategic Partnerships

Students are the main stakeholders. We are concerned about what is happening with them and how to make things better for them. The next set of stakeholders consists of families, teachers, community members, and education leaders. These are people who would be interested in or benefit from the work of the council. These stakeholders should be part of the processes of identifying what works, implementing solutions, and evaluating progress. Because we are focused on Black students, we need to think about partnerships that benefit, not exploit, them. What are some you know of?

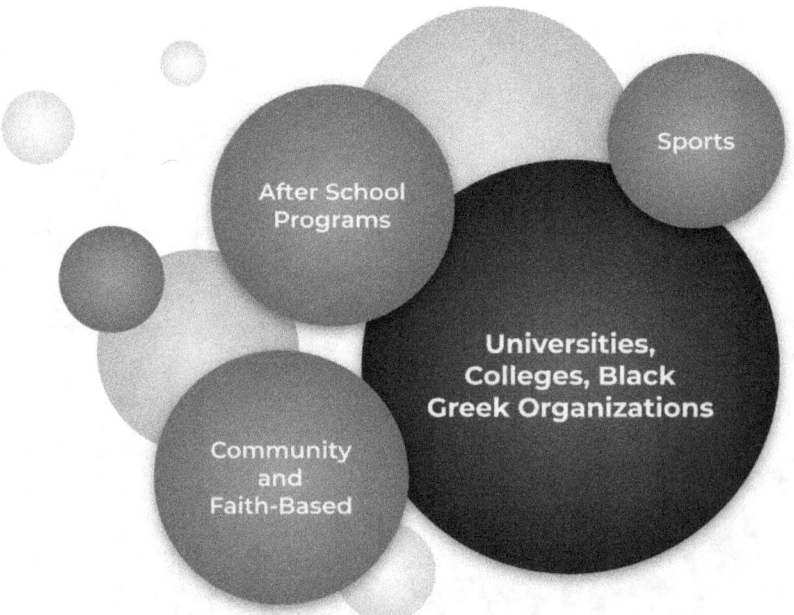

Strategic Partners

Supporting Sites

These are some things to consider as the council supports school sites.

- Clear expectations
    - What is the site expected to do?
    - How does it get resources?
    - Who is responsible?
    - Who are the key contacts?
- Leadership development
    - What is being done to develop people as leaders?
    - What resources do they need to do this well?
    - What are the needs?
    - What is helpful?
- Toolkits
    - What resources have you provided for the site to know the mission, vision, priorities, and important contacts within the organization and the district?
- Shared meetings
    - What is the plan to support sites with low numbers of Black scholars?
- Rotating venues/sharing space
    - What is the plan to collaborate across the district and where are places and spaces to meet off campus?

Reflections

If you already have a district council and are starting sites, how can you set the sites up for success?

If you are starting something new, what are all of the small and large pieces you'll need to know to get started? How can you give these to those who come after you in this work?

Interactive and Interdependent Work

Action

Based on what you have learned in this section, what are three specific, measurable, and realistic ways to set your current and future councils up for success?

1.

2.

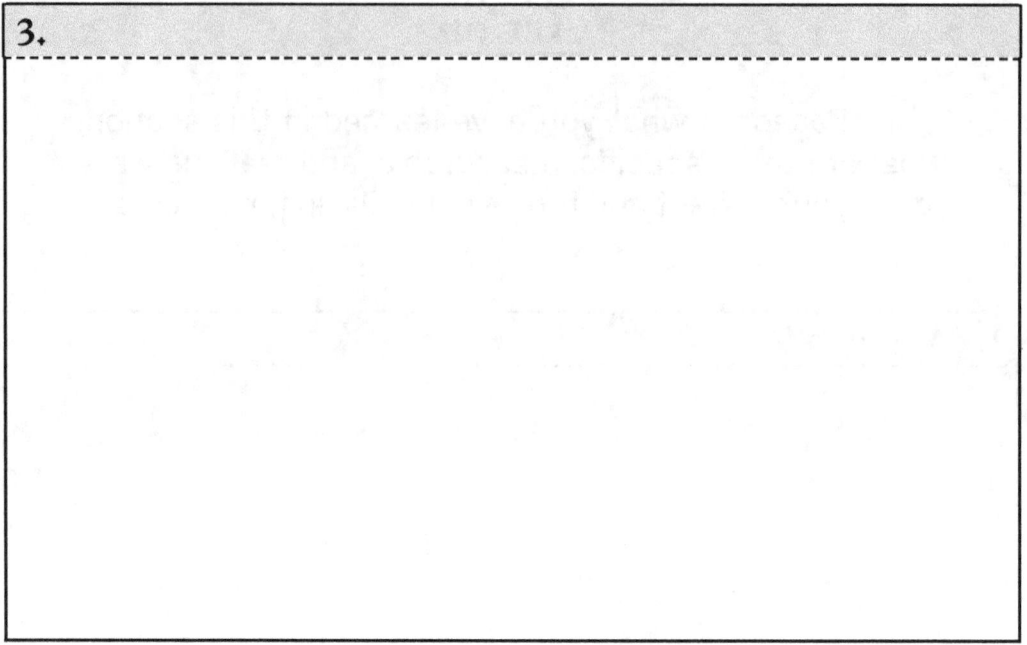

Engagement Strategies

"Black, Brown, and White families adapt to society and its value systems in different ways, in part because of the social class positions that members of each group experience"

(Willie et al., 2012, p.17).

My best advice about engagement strategies is to go to the spaces and places where the people reside, rest, play, worship, and leisure. Find authentic ways to collaborate to serve students. Again, it is not about getting families or scholars to a meeting at a school or district office. If we want to co-construct with families, we must do it where they feel safe so they can use their energies to create. Community and faith-based partnerships have been especially successful in bringing resources, advocacy, and support to Black families. Learn from faith-based and community organizations how to demonstrate respect and value for Black people. Space and place, resources and opportunities are not always available in schools, and they do not need to be. We want Black families and scholars connected to the curriculum, community, resources, and opportunities. We want the council to be a primary source of partnership for them so that our families and scholars do not have to go it alone or figure it out by themselves. All educational proceedings do not need to take place on district property or at school sites. Negotiate with schools and districts on where meetings can be held. Parent-teacher conferences, Individual Education Program (IEP) meetings, and other presentations do not have to be held on school sites either. Work as a team to develop situations that work for Black families.

Reflections

What are the names of the after-school programs on campus or in the district? Who are the contacts?

Who are the sports coaches and when can we meet with them?

What local fraternities, sororities, and parenting groups are focused on Black people, and how can we support what they are doing?

Interactive and Interdependent Work

Action

Based on what you read in this section, what are five specific and realistic goals for developing or enhancing strategic partnerships?

1.

2.

3.

4.

5.

What if Our District Has Not Initiated This Process?

There are several ways to begin the conversation about a BFAC in your district. I recommend starting with a small group of parents, community members, students, and teachers. I also recommend identifying board members who are concerned about the state of Black students. Community members may include members of local Black Greek organizations, faith-based organizations, and 100 Black Men of America. These groups have specific focuses and skill sets related to advocacy. As a group, you can use school data to create a compelling story about why a BFAC is a necessary support for Black students in the same way a district language learner advisory group for families of children with special needs is needed. Nationally most schools struggle to support the academic success and well-being of Black children and youth. Specific areas of concerns are math, language arts, advanced placement (AP) courses, and safety (psychological). University faculty can be very helpful in this process. There are a few, like myself, who study and organize around family and community involvement. They understand data and speak the language of educators. They can be useful in bridging the gap between the district and the community in understanding how a BFAC benefits Black students and supports schools in closing access and opportunity gaps.

It is important that those advocating for the BFAC understand its purpose and roles in schools. The message needs to be clear and consistent. Otherwise, schools may believe it is another version of PTA, and nothing could be further from the truth.

Expanding Your BFAC

I believe leadership development and strategic partnerships are keys to a council's ability to grow and thrive. There are some councils that are well-oiled machines. These more advanced BFACs should have a goal of creating a system that continues to develop new BFACs and new community leaders. This promotes the sustainability of the council.

In addition, more advanced BFACs can focus on expanding the quality and number of strategic partnerships. Advanced BFACs can also mentor less experienced BFACs. I believe there is power in numbers. I encourage BFACs to think about how they can gather regionally or by state a few times a year to discuss strategy, resources, and other avenues for supporting Black children and youth. BFACs are not intended to be the only course of action for Black students, and councils have limitations. BFACs are encouraged to think about resources, partners, actions, and initiatives outside of schools that may enhance Black student success and well-being. Moreover, although the council itself may not be able to engage in groups beyond the school or district, there is no rule that council members cannot create other informal or formal groups outside of schools.

Reflections

What are the strengths of your council?

How can the council strengthen its partnerships (vocation, business, finance, mentors)?

Who are the next leaders who can move the council forward?

What documents are in place to ensure the sustainability of the council? Do others know how to access them?

What are the measurable benefits of the council for Black students or families?

Action

Based on what you read in this section, what are five specific and realistic goals for expanding and sustaining your council?

1.

2.

3.

4.

5.

Conclusion

"It seems only reasonable that if under the present system we have gone backward or at least been kept from advancing to real freedom, it is high time to develop another sort of leadership with a different educational system"

(Woodson, 1933, p. 99).

    I appreciate you for recognizing the importance of this work. I believe we can make a difference one person, one family, one community, and one school at a time. It is my hope that your council takes this information and builds upon it. Expand. Grow. As you learn more, please continue to share and build. This is only the beginning.

    I invite those who are doing this work *and* are from historically marginalized communities to engage in self-care and preservation. This work can be difficult and discouraging, and at times it may feel like there is no progress. This work can also bring you great joy and be a source of justice and equity for children and families. Do not do it alone. Find a community and make a commitment to take care of yourself while you do this work.

Some of the practices that have helped me have been writing, walking, yoga, prayer, essential oils, naps, and increased social time with those I love. Find out what brings you joy and energizes you, and do that more as you do this work.

I will be praying for this work all over the world and that the condition and treatment of Black, Indigenous, Latina/o/x, Asian, and Pacific Islander people and those living in poverty and war will improve.

I invite you to visit my website, www.bridgesleadership.com, for ice breaker activities, a Black Family Advisory Playlist, toolkits, and bylaws.

Thank you.

Appendices

A. Sample BPC Agenda

I. Welcome

II. People

III. Introductions/ice breaker activity

IV. Mind-body practice

V. Updates

VI. Working groups

VII. Closing activity

B. Sample Guest Speaker Form

Thank you for your interest in sharing information with the Black Family Advisory Council. The purpose of Black family engagement is to help create more equitable schools and humanized conditions for Black students.

Please complete this form and give it to the BFAC leadership (site/district) at least 3 weeks prior to your requested speaker dates.

We communicated with the Council to get information about their questions or concerns related to the topic(s)?	Yes/No
Topics shared directly relate to Black Student Success.	Yes/No
There will be time built into the session for dialogue with the Council.	Yes/No
Graphics and visuals are shared that make the information clear.	Yes/No
Strategies are shared with BFAC about what can be done, or is being done to support Black students.	Yes/No
Topic(s)	
Duration of session (max 35 minutes)	
How will you make the session interactive?	

Appendices

C. Hospitality Checklist

Physical Space

- Is there someone there to greet people?
- Does everyone know someone?
- Are the aesthetics of the culture (art, music) represented in the space?
- Are there people who look like BFAC families there/leading?
- Is the room set up in a way that promotes interaction and relationships?
- Is there time for people to connect before or after the gathering?
- Is there a place for people's children?

Emotional Space

- Members are given space to share how they feel
- Judgement about other people's feelings are withheld
- People are encouraged to connect with others outside of gatherings
- Resources are shared that support families and students
- Members never leave without knowing someone

Intellectual Space

- Is the space free of judgement?
- Are there opportunities for people to share their stories?
- People's ideas and concerns are recognized and acknowledged
- BFAC members are invited to co-construct and co-develop

Spiritual Space

- We recognize the BFAC families are diverse and bring various religious world views
- People are invited to integrate their faith, and spiritual practices in how they support their children
- Members are encouraged to strengthen their spiritual lives

Appendices

D. Theory and Practice

"What we do is more important than what we say or what we say we believe."

—bell hooks

The principles and practices espoused in this book have a solid foundation in theory. Theories are a system of ideas or suppositions, that intend to help to explain something. The frameworks, models and practices promoted in this book are supported by well-developed and rigorously tested theories. Because this book is intended for easy use, the author has connected the practices, and principles with theory or theoretical-based frameworks and models for you. You are encouraged to read more on the theories to ensure they are the ideas you want to promote.

Practices/Principles	Theory/Framework	Theory/Framework Explanation
Schools working with families to form partnerships that support students.	Overlapping Spheres of Influence Model (Epstein, 1995)	The school, family, and community influence children. The closer those spheres come together to support the child, the better.
Creating safe spaces for Black families and students in schools.	Maslow Hierarchy of Needs (Maslow, 1943)	A person's psychological and physical need for safety must be met in order from them to self-actualize in any given environment.

Practices/Principles	Theory/Framework	Theory/Framework Explanation
Co-identifying issues and constructing experiences with Black families that lead to problem-solving.	Du Boisian Framework (Serrano, 2018)	William Edward Burghart Du Bois, or W.E.B. Du Bois, was known for using extensive field work in and with communities to solve social issues in the Black community. Three tenets guide community-based and participatory research: (a) collaboration between students, families, communities, and professors; (b) the utilization of multiple research methods and disseminating approaches; (c) an emphasis on social justice and change that benefits the participants and their communities; (d) centering lived experience over formal education/positions; disrupting hierarchies (Strand et al., 2003).

Practices/Principles	Theory/Framework	Theory/Framework Explanation
The importance of invitation, attention to the nuances of race and culture in involvement and engagement, and valuing many types of involvement.	Hoover-Dempsey, & Sandler Model (Hoover-Dempsey et al., 2005)	Families use encouragement, modeling, reinforcement, and instruction as mechanisms for involvement during involvement activities. Forms of involvement include: values, goals, expectations, aspirations, activities at home, communication with the school, and involvement with activities at school.
Centering the knowledge, practice and lifeways of Black families in the work of supporting Black students.	Black Cultural Capital (Carter, 2003)	Black students develop their own forms of cultural capital. Their capital is shared across class with other Black and African American people. It is shaped by music, art, cultural tastes, expressive styles and interactions.

Equitable By Design

Acknowledgements

I want to take a moment to acknowledge the people and places that made this project possible.

People

I begin with the families, people, and community members who first taught me. They taught me the importance of morals and values and showed me the power of families, neighborhoods, and communities when they work towards common goals.

I first want to thank my parents, Omie Mills-Cormier and Lawrence J. Cormier, their parents Ruthie Mills, Johnnie Mills, Ella M. Washington, and Ben Washington. Their models of hard-work, high value for education, entrepreneurship, and well-being, concern for and connections to the community, and applications of faith gave me the mindsets and tools to engage with this project in ways that are beneficial to others.

I started and finished this book in the middle of dual pandemics, increased structural racism and COVID-19. For approximately 8 months, I was not able to physically connect with my parents and most of my family (six siblings, nieces, and nephews) in ways that promoted generational healing. In other words, for exactly 8 months, I was not able to write. Although I had plenty of projects, completed new IRBs, collected new data, and analyzed previous data, the pain and fear of watching the world become more chaotic and unjust, coupled with knowing that hundreds of thousands of people around the world lost their lives, including the parents of my two dear friends, immobilized me.

Watching my parents during this time gave me hope. Their decision to prioritize their physical, spiritual, financial and emotional health prior to COVID-19 proved beneficial. It lessened the negative impacts of COVID-19 on both them and their children. They embraced Zoom and video calls with friends and family as a means to connect and to do so often. They even created online Yoga and Qigong classes for elders. Twice a week, for one hour, they virtually met with elders from across their city and state to engage in physical activity. I know that for many of these elders, it was also a means of social emotional support, as many were isolated from their families and friends, too. Because my parents embraced technology, we were able to share laughter, effectively communicate, celebrate special occasions, share stories, and encourage one another virtually. After some months, knowing that I could see my parents again physically and that they would survive COVID-19, I was able to move from survival mode to thriving once again.

This book would not exist without the leadership, knowledge, wisdom, expertise, gifts, discernments, and experiences of families of Black students, and their respective communities. They have shaped and guided the contents of this book. Black families and their communities have persevered with grace even in the face of great discouragement and adversities. They have shared their deepest joys and greatest challenges with me. They have shared their gifts, expertise, talents, time, energy and resources to help me learn what it means to create equitable partnerships in schools.

Acknowledgements

They have forgiven, loved, and reconciled in the quest for safe places for their children to learn and receive a meaningful education. I am deeply grateful to the community leaders, faith leaders, and organizers that have invited me in to work alongside them as we worked for common goals. I am appreciative of all of the university leaders, faculty, and staff for their support. A special thank you to the educational practitioners, some of which wear dual hats as both family members and educators. If not for their courage to take a stand in the face of possible job loss, and other stereotypes, this book would not be as comprehensive as it is. I also want to thank the administrative assistants, student workers, instructional assistants, and students who shared their time, organizational skills, and perspective with me because they believe in this work.

Embracing, developing, and maintaining a network of support has been a strategy to cope with stress. My network of support during this project was deep and wide. Stephanie Y. Evans in her 2021 book, *Black Women's Yoga History*, points out that systemic violence as a stressor cannot be addressed with individual self-care methods. "Changing the system requires a collective effort" (p. 90). Thus, I want to offer thanks to my university and college leadership for being a support and not a hindrance as I wrote this book. I want to thank my sisters, who have been best friends of choice for over 30 years: Margaux Johnson, Alexis Cormier, Diane Flowers, Camisha Nicole, and Kashi Cormier Walmer. These ladies have been a listening ear, an objective perspective, prayer partners, cheerleaders, branding and marketing experts, and anything else I've needed. I am grateful for my academic tribe, Drs. Rema Reynolds, Cheryl Matias, Kimberly White-Smith, Regina Trammel, Amber Parks, and Ie May Freeman. These are the folks I look to when I feel depleted and discouraged by the academy and all of its fixings. They checked on me. Sent food during a difficult time, and made space for fun in the middle of dual pandemics. They gave me strategies, prayers, encouragement and the connections I needed to persevere. To my special sisters—Maisha, Maia and Katrina—it has been 26 years and your support during COVID-19 was special. I needed those heart and soul connections. Thank you. I would be remiss if I did not state my gratitude for my local chapter, Pasadena Alumnae of Delta Sigma Theta. It was my elder sorors who prayed for me and checked in on me when our family endured a life-shock. These ladies provided spiritual and sisterly connections that uplifted my spirits as we served our communities together during devastating times. To my Sunday morning Bible study group, you all kept me thinking and speaking faith. To the elders of the group, thank you for letting me know that you have been where I am and reassuring me that it will all work for my good.

To Henry Latunde and Monet Latunde—I am so grateful for your time, energy, and gifts that you shared with me to make this book possible. Henry, you provided the best edits and reads. You made great recommendations, as you know this work as much as I do. Thank you for the long brainstorming walks and great ideas. Monet, thank you for helping me to research, and for telling me, *"Mom, you know this. Be confident."* Thank you for sharing your gifts of art with me and the world.

Aranza Perez-Cano, your organizational guidance and love for the community helped me to see my blind spots. I appreciate your input into this project and your belief in me and this book. To Ann Byers, thank you for helping me to put my best foot forward by providing your editing expertise. We have been working together since the dissertation, and you are more than a writing partner. You are a prayer partner and encouragement. Thank you.

Acknowledgements

To the Mindful Leaders Project group: Drs. Niki Elliott, Akida Long, Sunny, Amy, and Kate. Being able to connect with you on a regular basis to reflect, breathe, discharge, plan, and strategize as I wrote this book gave me energy. The friendships we developed as we served were deeply satisfying and reduced isolation and periodic feelings of depletion. Thank you.

Places

To Riverside County Office of Education, Pasadena Unified Schools, Pasadena Unified School District, Mt. Zion Assemblies (Fresno, CA), and Bethesda (Fresno, CA) you have been a safe place for the families, educators, community members, and myself to learn and try new things. You recognized the power of Black families and their connections to one another and their communities, and centralized their knowledge and practices in order to support Black students. I have learned more from you than time I have to write about it.

I am a product of Fresno, CA. West Fresno (Dr. Martin Luther King & Jensen) to be exact. This place, nestled in the Central Valley of California, has provided me with a firm foundation. I was able to benefit from the positive contributions of my neighborhoods, local churches, parks, recreation centers, schools and businesses. It is my first experience with identity, race, faith, class, gender and the intersection of them all. This place provided me with so many great models of success in education, leadership, politics, and business and in people who look like me. Much gratitude to West Fresno Christian Academy. This is the place where I had my first sleepovers, met my first best friends, like Camisha Nicole, and held my first paid positions as an employee. It is where I was affirmed and protected daily, monthly, and always.

I am a proud graduate of Kings River Community College (KRCC) AKA (Reedley College), CSU, Sacramento, Clark Atlanta University, and Nova Southeastern University. Two of these places are special to me. KRCC is where other Black people—Dr. Christine Johnson-McPhall and Cal Johnson specifically—in positions of power reached out and supported me in a variety of ways. It is also where it occurred to me how low the expectations are for Black students in college and how little support is provided. Clark Atlanta University was a beacon of light; it is where I found a home away from home. The School of Education provided me with a top-notch education, preparing me to do exceptionally well in all certification tests and in my profession. It was Drs. Sara Bealings, Veda Jairrels, and Patricia Ward that showed me yet again, it would be other Black women that would support, guide, heal, and protect me; it was on their shoulders I would stand. I am eternally grateful for you all.

About the Author

Dr. Yvette C. Latunde is a Co-Director for the Center for Educational Equity and Intercultural Research (CEEIR) and Professor in the Doctor of Organizational Leadership Program at the University of La Verne. She is the founder of Bridges Leadership and Education Services, LLC. An educator for over two decades, she has traveled widely to share the good news about the strengths, capacities, and capabilities of students, their families, and their communities. She is an international speaker, author, and community servant who enjoys yoga, writing, walking, and spending time in nature. She is the daughter of Omie M. & Larry Cormier; sister of Jacques, Margaux, Tristian, Kashi, and Alexis; mother of Jazmone, Monet, and Karsten; friend to Diane, Camisha-Nicole, and her sisters. Yvette loves God and believes that with Him all things are possible when you believe and act in obedience.

Her areas of expertise include: Family Engagement, Black Family Engagement with schools, Neurodiversity in the Workplace, Inclusive Leadership, and Home-Schools-Community Partnerships.

References

Allen, Q., & White-Smith, K. (2018). "That's why I say stay in school": Black mothers' parental involvement, cultural wealth, and exclusion in their son's [sic] schooling. *Urban Education*, 53(3), 409-435. https://doi.org/10.1177/0042085917714516

Arrington, E. G., & Stevenson, H. C. (2006). *Final report for the Success of African American Students (SAAS) in independent schools project*. https://repository.upenn.edu/gse_pubs/23

Battiste, M. (2002). Indigenous knowledge and pedagogy in first nations education: A literature review with recommendations, 1-69. National Working Group on Education.

Blackstock, Cindy. (2011). The emergency of the breath of life theory. *Journal of Social Work Values and Ethics*, 8, 1.

Bridges, B. K., Awokoya, J. T., & Messano, F. (2012). *Done to us, not with us: African American parent perceptions of K-12 education*. Washington, DC: Frederick D. Patterson Research Institute. https://files.eric.ed.gov/fulltext/ED573649.pdf

Carter, P. (2003). "Black" cultural capital, status positioning, and schooling conflicts for low-income African American youth. *Social Problems*, 50(1), 136-155.

Epstein, J. L. (1995). School/family/community partnerships: Caring for the children we share. *Phi Delta Kappan*, 76, 701-712.

Evans, S. Y. (2021). *Black women's yoga history: Memoirs of inner peace*. State University of New York.

Garcia, J., Shirley, V., Windchief, S., & San Pedro, T. (2020). Pedagogy of solidarity. In A.E. Shield, D. Paris, R. Paris, & T. San Pedro *Education in Movement Spaces*. Indigenous and Decolonizing Student in Education series. Routledge.

Hill, R. B. (2003). *The strengths of Black families* (2nd ed.). University Press of America.

Hoover-Dempsey, K. V., & Sandler, H. M. (1995). Parental involvement in children's education: Why does it make a difference? *Teachers College Record*, 97(2), 310–331.

Hoover-Dempsey, K. V., Walker, J. M. T., Sandler, H. M., Whetsel, D., Green, C. L., Wilkins, A. S., & Clossan, K. (2005). Why do parents become involved? Research findings and implications. *Elementary School Journal*, 106(2), 105-130.

Ishimaru, A. M. (2019). *Just schools: Building Equitable Collaborations with Families and Communities*. Multicultural Education Series. Teachers College Press.

Jeynes, W. H. (2003). The effects of Black and Hispanic 12th graders living in intact families and being religious on their academic achievement. *Urban Education*, 38(1), 35–57. https://doi.org/10.1177/0042085902238685

Khalifa, M., (2018). *Culturally responsive school leadership*. Harvard Education Press.

Latunde, Y. C. (2017). *Research in parental involvement: Methods and strategies for education and psychology*. Palgrave-Macmillan.

Maslow, A. H. (1943). A theory of human motivation. *Psychological Review*, 50(4), 370–396. https://doi.org/10.1037/h0054346

McKnight, J., & Block, P. (2012). *The abundant community: Awakening the power of families and neighborhoods*. Berrett-Koehler Publishers, Inc.

References

Olson, K. (2014). *The invisible classroom: Relationships, neuroscience & mindfulness in school.* W. W. Norton & Company.

Pushor, D. (2017, Winter). *Family centric schools: Creating a place for all parents.* Education Canada, Vol. 27(4).

Serrano, U. (2018). Symposium of W. E. B. Du Bois: The Philadelphia Negro: W. E. B. Du Bois and community-based research. *Section Culture*, 30(1). https://asaculturesection.org/2018/07/22/symposium-on-w-e-b-du-bois-the-philadelphia-negro-w-e-b-du-bois-and-community-based-research/

Steidle, G. K. (2017). Leading from within: Conscious social change and mindfulness for social innovation. MIT Press.

Willie, C. V., & Reddick, R. J. (2010). *A new look at Black families* (6th ed.). Rowman & Littlefield.

Woodson, C. G. (1933). *The mis-education of the Negro.* Tribeca Books.

Index

A

Advisement 57

Advisory council 13, 57

Anti-Blackness xviii, 45

B

Black families i, iii, iv, xi, xii, xiii, xiv, xvii, 1, 7, 11, 17, 19, 20, 21, 23, 30, 33, 37, 40, 41, 45, 46, 49, 55, 71, 85, 101, 108, 116, 123, 139, 140, 141, 152, 153

Black Family Advisory Council (BFAC) 1, 2, 7, 8, 11, 25, 45, 57, 69, 81, 114, 126, 127, 136, 137, 138

Black Lives Matter 23

Black students iv, xi, xiii, xiv, xviii, 5, 6, 8, 13, 21, 23, 24, 25, 37, 45, 58, 76, 77, 79, 80, 81, 82, 85, 86, 89, 93, 94, 97, 98, 99, 108, 118, 126, 127, 128, 130, 136, 141

Board approval 57, 58. *See also* Board of Education

Board of Education 13, 59, 60, 61, 109, 126

Bylaws 66, 68, 134

C

Capacity building 5, 68, 69

Communities i, xi, xii, xiii, xiv, xviii, 2, 3, 5, 6, 23, 30, 40, 103, 116, 140

Connections xiv, 19, 35, 41, 46, 49, 97, 112, 113

D

Data 8, 25, 37, 58, 59, 60, 61, 69, 79, 80, 81, 94, 116, 126, 127

District advisory 57, 58, 92

E

Engagement 1, 4, 7, 8, 9, 116, 122

Engagement strategies 122

Equity 4, 8, 83, 133

Every Student Succeeds Act 3, 7

Evidenced-based practices xii, 80, 82

External actions 41

F

Faith-based partnerships 122

Family engagement 2, 4, 7, 11, 13, 14, 17, 19, 83, 97, 136

G

Goals xix, 11, 37, 40, 43, 49, 54, 58, 61, 65, 66, 70, 77, 79, 80, 82, 84, 85, 88, 92, 105, 111, 115, 117, 125, 131, 141

Guest speakers 36

H

Healing-centered practices 21, 69, 74, 79, 82

Hospitality 20, 29, 30, 32, 137

I

Individuals with Disabilities Education Act 3

Instruction 74, 141

Index

Interactive iv, xvii, 25, 26, 27, 28, 107, 108, 114, 136

Internal development 41. *See also* Internal work

Internal work 4

L

Leadership xii, 7, 14, 33, 46, 57, 68, 69, 79, 82, 85, 92, 127, 133, 136, 152

Leadership development 69, 127

Literacy 64. *See also* Racial literacy

Local Control and Accountability Plan (LCAP) 69, 79, 85

M

Meetings xvii, 3, 4, 11, 13, 24, 35, 57, 58, 68, 69, 98, 107, 113, 114, 116, 117, 119, 123

Messaging 20, 97, 98, 101, 114, 116

Mindfulness 21, 41, 69, 153

Monthly meetings 92

N

Non-academic factors 91, 96

P

Parent advisory group 58

Policies iv, xv, 1, 4, 68

Priorities 58, 59, 66, 79, 80, 107, 115, 119

R

Racial literacy 64

Racism 13, 40, 45, 55, 82

Index

Relationships iv, xvii, 23, 33, 63, 85, 88, 113, 137

Representation 6, 20, 25, 37, 38

S

Safety xi, 6, 12, 30, 31, 32, 40, 80, 81, 127, 139

Self-care 69, 112

Site advisories 58

Site plan 79, 81, 82

Space xv, 24, 26, 33, 35, 39, 40, 46, 57, 112, 113, 115, 119, 137, 138

Strategic partnerships xi, 116, 125, 127

Strengths xiv, xv, xvii, 11, 12, 24, 40, 103, 104, 105, 128, 152

Structural racism 13, 40, 45, 82. *See also* Racism

Structure 12, 46, 66, 67, 69, 92, 115

Student well-being. *See also* Well-being

T

Teaching xviii, 12, 14, 36, 74, 86

Team xii, 15, 55, 64, 66, 69, 112, 123

Theory xi, xii, xiv, 74, 94, 139, 151, 152

Training 21, 57, 83, 85

W

Well-being xi, xii, xiii, 5, 8, 70, 76, 77, 79, 91, 127, 128

White fragility 55. *See also* Whiteness

White House Executive Order on Advancing Racial Equity and Support for Underserved Communities 1

Index

White House Initiative on Educational Excellence for African Americans 1, 2

Whiteness 21, 40

Y

Yearly practice ideas 79

www.ingramcontent.com/pod-product-compliance
Lightning Source LLC
Chambersburg PA
CBHW081744100526
44592CB00015B/2299